THE EMOTIONALLY EMPOWERED WOMAN

A Guide to Becoming an Emotionally Aware
and Empowered Woman

BY
DR. EVELYN OKPANACHI

All rights reserved. No part of this publication may be reproduced, stored in a retrieval system or transmitted, in any form or by any means without the prior permission in writing of the author or as expressly permitted by law, or under terms agreed with the appropriate reprographics rights organisation.

Enquiries concerning reproduction outside the scope of the above should be sent to the author. You must not circulate this book in any other binding or cover, and you must impose this same condition on any acquirer.

In no way is it legal to reproduce, duplicate, or transmit any part of this document in either electronic means or in printed format. Recording of this publication is strictly prohibited and any storage of this document is not allowed unless with written permission from the publisher.

This document is geared towards providing exact and reliable information in regards to the topic and issue covered. Under no circumstances will any legal responsibility or blame be held against the publisher for any reparation, damages, or monetary loss due to the information herein, either directly or indirectly.

Copyright © Evelyn Okpanachi 2023

The moral right of the author has been asserted.
Printed in the United Kingdom
Produced By Bytels Publishing

Dedicated to All Women

ABOUT THE AUTHOR

Dr. Evelyn Okpanachi wears many hats but her core goal is to empower women to achieve the next level. Over the years, Dr. Evelyn has built multiple businesses, and hence the term serial entrepreneur has been used when describing her. She is a business and life coach who supports women to curate the life they desire.

As part of her journey to empower women, she has stepped into the realm of empowering with action through her action-packed Masterclasses in Africa, UAE, and the UK. She has founded groups for women who believe that they are integral to society and relevant to building happy and strong communities. Dr. Evelyn is the author of a series of eBooks and blogs but more recently *"The Habit Tracker", "Growth Mindset for Entrepreneurs" and "Productivity Secrets for Entrepreneurs"*.

Dr. Evelyn empowers through action and believes we rise by lifting others. She often remarks, *"another woman is never my competition ... I believe in sistership."* Her aim has always been to ensure women reach their full potential and break barriers she didn't think she could.

She is the co-founder of RIAPS, a non-profit organization that stands against poverty and is passionate about eradicating poverty in local communities.

She is also the co-founder of Royal Leadership Consults, which empowers the next generation of leaders to lead with empathy and compassion.

APPRECIATION

My deep appreciation to all who see the value and importance of an emotionally empowered woman.

I am thankful for my late father Mr Cosmas Chukwudi and my husband Dr. James Okpanachi, who have supported and believed in women empowerment. I am grateful for my husband who encouraged me to write this book.

To my daughters who are growing to be emotionally empowered women and my mother Mrs Margaret Chukwudi who is the epitome of the emotionally empowered woman.

To the group of women who I regard as sisters in Victorious Ladies where we support each other's growth.

PUBLISHER'S NOTE

Are you a woman who feels like you are stuck in the rut of your emotional life? Do you desire to find ways that will help you become more emotionally aware and lead you towards emotional empowerment but do not know where to start? This specially crafted guide will help you discover strategies for becoming an emotionally empowered woman. It will assist in changing your emotional reactions and perspectives as you learn to be aware of them and take more control.

This book focuses on transforming women into emotionally empowered women away from the emotional stereotype denoted to them. It is a self-help guide derived from Dr. Evelyn Okpanachi's power-packed masterclass sessions on emotional empowerment for women. This guide/book helps women embrace and understand how to master their emotions for success.

This guide will equip you with the necessary tools and practices that lead you to more emotional awareness while detecting the positive, and also the negative emotions that you may want to change through the control of your emotional expressions. Here, we discuss the most common questions women encounter in their journey to emotional awareness and empowerment:

- Understanding how our emotions affect our actions as women
- Knowing how to break free from the emotional woman stigma
- Understanding what it means to be an emotionally empowered woman
- Embracing and understanding how to master our emotions as women for success
- Grasping the importance of taking care of yourself emotionally
- Gaining knowledge on how to become more emotionally empowered
- Receiving tips for staying emotionally balanced and healthy
- Understanding the benefits of being an emotionally empowered woman

This guide focuses on the emotional triggers of daily life that cause emotional feats. You will learn how to manage these emotions turning them into positive responses thus maximizing the enjoyment of your life.

> ➢ Join others who have made a conscious decision to learn how to take control of their lives by seeking to understand their emotions and embarking on the journey to becoming Emotionally Empowered women.

➢ Discover the numerous routes to emotional transformation and become an emotionally empowered woman today!

NOTES FROM READERS AND STUDENTS FROM THE EMOTIONALLY EMPOWERED WOMAN MASTERCLASS.

Masterclass with Dr. Evelyn Okpanachi

"I did the masterclass with Dr. Evelyn last year, and I thoroughly enjoyed it. I counted my blessings and achievements in 2020 with her guidance, which enabled me to think through my immediate priorities for 2021. I gained clarity on issues that held me back in the past from truly living up to my potential and more. With her coaching, I set myself SMART goals and actions for 2021, and I have already seen results. I am now able to push myself and work harder. Dr. Evelyn is now coaching to help me achieve my short-term goals and work towards the long-term ones. Dr. Evelyn helped me dig deep and focus on areas that I needed to work on and focus on to see the changes I desire."

Koffo Abayomi-Bassey

"Thank you very much for offering a wonderful service. It was a great Mastermind, and I learned a lot over the four weeks; the sessions really got me thinking deeply about my goals in a realistic and motivating way. I value the time and know that the session will help me make great progress in my life. Thank you."

Muka Anyado

"I thought this was an excellent session, and I felt privileged for the opportunity to be part of it. The sessions were well thought out, and you learn something new about yourself every week. It forced me to identify what may be hindrances in my life and where I can do better.

The course was varied, so that kept my attention. I never felt bored, nor was I distracted by other things around me. Getting homework at the end of every session was so helpful, so this forced me to think about mindfulness continuously until the next session. I believe this to be helpful, as it makes you aware of what is going on in your life and being able to put what you have learned from each session in your daily life."
Esame Matthews

"I thoroughly enjoyed the mastermind and was glad to be part of the different sessions. The content was excellent and concisely laid out. Dr. Evelyn Okpanachi clearly knew her subject well and delivered it adequately.

I thought the mastermind was powerfully delivered and left me with many takeaway points to apply in my everyday life. I would definitely recommend it to all irrespective of their background, social status, and career."

Ijay Egbe

TABLE OF CONTENTS

About The Author i
Appreciation iii
Publisher's Note iv
Notes From Readers and Students from The Emotionally
Empowered Woman Masterclass. vii

PART 1: Understanding Emotions 1

Chapter 1: Understanding Our Emotions 2

What are Emotions? 2
How are Emotions Formed? 3
Is the Theory of Constructed Emotions Real? 4
Types of Emotions 8
Emotions Are Changeable 18
Coping with Negative Emotions 19
When Is One Emotional? 27
Emotional Triggers 28

How To Recognize Triggers 29

How Do Our Emotions Affect Our Actions? 30

Male Emotions vs. Female Emotions 37

Why Do Our Emotions Hold Us Back? 40

Which Emotions Are Holding Us Back? 41

Facts about Emotions 42

Chapter 2: Women and their Emotions 49

Women As Emotional Beings 49

Motherhood and Parenting 50

Singlehood 51

Married Life 52

Dealing With the Death of a Loved One 54

Divorce or Separation 54

Abuse: Physical, Emotional, Sexual 55

Hormonal Changes and Menopause 55

Emotional Baggage 56

Chapter 3: The Emotional Woman Stigma 61

What Emotional Stigmas Do Women Face? 61

Breaking Free from the Emotional Woman Stigma 63

Chapter 4: How Beliefs Affect Our Emotions 66

Our Beliefs Play a Huge Role 66

Be Aware of Your Own Personal Beliefs and How They
Affect You 67

Beliefs about Beauty, Relationships, Motherhood, and Work 68

We Must Question Our Beliefs 70

How To Change Negative Beliefs 71

Chapter 5: The Influence of Culture on Our Emotions 73

How Different Cultures Affect Emotions 73

Why Are Emotions Cultural Phenomena? 75

Cultural Differences in Emotional Arousal Level 81

Chapter 6: Emotions and Our Mental Health 85

Clarifying Mental Health 85

Reducing the Risk Factors of Mental Health Conditions 86

Good Mental Health Is Instrumental to Our Emotions and How We Act! 87

Emotional Health 93

Chapter 7: Identifying and Differentiating Between Emotional Needs and Emotions and Needs 96

What Are Emotional needs 96

Emotions and Needs 102

The Basic Concept of Needs 105

Emotional Intelligence (EI) 108

Emotional Differentiation 110

PART 2: What is Emotional Empowerment 112

Chapter 1: What Emotional Empowerment is NOT 113

What is Low EQ? 113

How To Know When You Have Low EQ 114

1. They Must Always Be 'Right' and Are Highly Opinionated 114

2. They Lack Empathy and Behave Insensitively. 115

3. They Have Narcissistic Tendencies: Self-Centeredness 115

4. They Blame Others For Their Problems and Lack Accountability 116

5. Unpredictable Emotional Outbursts and Poor Self-Regulation 117

Improving Emotional Intelligence 119

How to Embrace Emotions and Get to the Next Level 121

3 Tips for Dealing with Difficult Emotions in A Healthy Way 122

Chapter 2: Emotional Maturity 125

What Emotional Maturity Looks Like 125

How Women Can Become Emotionally Mature 130

Five Benefits of Having High Emotional Maturity as a Woman 132

Chapter 3: Women Who Have Shown Great Emotional Empowerment 135

World Class Emotionally Empowered Women 135

Chapter 4: Steven Covey's Take on Emotions 147
How The 7 Habits of Highly Effective People affect Emotions 147

PART 3: How to Be an Emotionally Empowered Woman 152

Chapter 1: Emotional Self-Care 153
What is Emotional Self-Care? 153
Why You Need to Practice Emotional Self-Care 154
How to Practice Emotional Self-Care 155

Chapter 2: Being Emotionally Empowered 158
Who Is the Emotionally Empowered Woman? 158
How to Be More Emotionally Empowered 160

Chapter 3: Communication and Emotional Empowerment of Women 169
What is Effective Communication? 169
Effective Ways of Communicating Emotions 171
When Is Communication Critical for Emotional Empowerment? 175

Chapter 4: How to be Assertive for Emotional Empowerment 183
What is Being Assertive? 183

Benefits of Assertiveness 185

Habits You Can Adopt to Become Assertive 187

Chapter 5: Celebrating Emotional Empowerment in Women **194**

Chapter 6: Your Emotional Intelligence Quiz **198**

Conclusion 209

References 211

PART 1:
UNDERSTANDING EMOTIONS

CHAPTER 1:

UNDERSTANDING OUR EMOTIONS

We all know that women are emotionally strong. They have to be in order to deal with the challenges of life. But have you ever considered your emotions? Where do they come from? Why do you feel and react in specific ways to different situations? What is it that makes our emotions so strong? And how can we tap into that power and strength? In this chapter, we will understand our emotions so we can become emotionally empowered women.

What are Emotions?

Emotions are a source of information that can help you understand what is happening around you and are 'lower level' responses. They first appear in the brain's subcortical areas, such as the amygdala and ventromedial prefrontal cortices. These areas are in charge of generating biochemical reactions that immediately impact your physical state. Emotions are encoded in our DNA and are thought to have evolved to help us respond quickly to various environmental threats, similar to our "fight or flight" response. The amygdala is essential in releasing neurotransmitters necessary for memory, which explains why emotional memories are frequently stronger and easier to recall.

Emotions are therefore the psychological states of response to neurophysiological changes usually associated with behavioural responses, thoughts, and a degree of pleasure or displeasure. Psychologists define emotions as a complex mental reaction characterized by physical and psychological changes that influence thought and behaviour linked to a variety of psychological phenomena such as temperament, personality, mood, and motivation.

As conscious mental responses (such as anger or fear) that are subjectively distinguished as an intense sensation, they are usually directed toward a specific object and are generally accompanied by physiological and behavioural changes in the body.

Emotions are produced when the brain interprets what is going on around us using memories, thoughts, and beliefs, an occurrence that influences how we feel and behave. This process has an impact on all of our decisions in some way. It is natural to make emotional decisions.

How are Emotions Formed?

We can look at how emotions form in two ways, depending on whether we use the traditional view or the Theory of Constructed Emotion.

The traditional view holds that the brain is pre-wired with neurons dedicated to a specific emotion and is triggered by something in the environment, like a little bomb. Once activated, the neurons create a fingerprint that identifies the emotion, such as a specific facial expression that is universally recognized. Early emotion scientists, for example, were drawn to a theory of universality: Emotions are innate, biologically driven reactions to specific challenges and opportunities shaped by evolution to help humans survive. This is why people in danger appear to experience fear regardless of habitat or culture, and they flee.

Parents who look at their children report feeling love, which encourages selfless caregiving. These researchers set out to document the felt experiences, expressive behaviors, and patterns of emotion comprehension in Western and non-Western cultures and discovered many commonalities.

According to the Theory of Constructed Emotion, emotions are formed based on prior experience. The brain creates emotion by using previous emotional experiences to predict and explain incoming sensory inputs and guide action. It uses the incoming input to confirm or change its prediction and is true for hearing, taste, vision, and all other senses. Lisa Feldman-Barrett also contends that emotions are learned responses based on our experiences and prior knowledge rather than inborn, automatic responses.

Is the Theory of Constructed Emotions Real?

Yes, it is! The Theory of Constructed Emotion provides a revolutionary new perspective on emotions, their origin, and how they shape our lives. In a 2017 publication, Bryce states that the Theory of Constructed Emotion contradicts many of our most deeply held beliefs about how human emotions work. The theory was explicitly discussed by Dr. Lisa Feldman Barrett, a psychology professor and neuroscientist at Northeastern University, in her best-selling book *How Emotions Are Made* in 2017.

It emphasizes, for example, that:

- Emotions are not hardwired in a primitive, "reptilian" part of the brain.
- Facial expressions or any other physiological measurement cannot detect emotions.
- No "universal" emotions are shared by all people, nations, or cultures.
- There are no separate parts of the brain dedicated to different emotions (such as the amygdala for fear).
- Emotions aren't "reactions" to outside events.

The name of the Theory of Constructed Emotion comes from its central premise: emotions are concepts created by the brain. Take a moment to consider your brain. It collects information from your eyes, ears, nose, skin, and mouth. This information is useful, but it is also ambiguous. It will have to be interpreted.

The brain is constantly attempting to make sense of the information it receives. Using past experiences as a guide is one of the simplest ways to do so. It can save time and energy if it matches the current experience with a previous memory. However, considering thousands of old memories one at a time would take far too long.

Instead, the brain makes use of concepts. A concept is a condensed version of hundreds or thousands of previous experiences. For instance, instead of remembering every encounter, you've ever had with a "table," your brain stores a concept of a table. When you see a table again, your brain only needs to match it with this concept to understand what it's seeing.

Concepts are categories and label your brain creates to help you make sense of the world around you. When you see something new, your brain asks, "What is this like?" rather than "What is this?" In other words, your brain constantly attempts to categorize everything you see. It is much easier to do this than to figure it out from scratch.

Dr. Barrett uses the term "simulation" rather than "interpretation" because the brain does not simply observe incoming data from the outside world passively. As a result, its decisions would be extremely slow, potentially jeopardizing our survival. The brain begins reacting even before it has received all of the data - it creates a "simulation" or prediction of what it believes will happen next to act faster. Essentially, the brain is constantly making the best guess it can of what is about to happen and then preparing to act on that guess.

Our mental simulations are more real to us than the physical world. What we see, hear, touch, taste, and smell are world simulations, not reactions to it. We may believe that events shape our perceptions of the world, but most of what we see is based on our internal predictions. The information we receive through our senses influences our perceptions and the resulting emotions.

Key Takeaways That Make the Theory of Constructed Emotion Practical and Realistic

1) The classical view of emotions still reigns supreme today, despite scientific evidence to the contrary.

We often think of emotions in our society as something you can't control, almost like a reflex. This traditional viewpoint holds that emotions are irrational reflexes left over from our evolution. The traditional view does not work because we can express every emotion differently. This is because each emotional response is unique to the situation, as opposed to us experiencing a few recurring emotions. As Barret suggests, while societies may have expressive patterns, there is no universal brain response to each emotion.

2) We spontaneously create emotions based on sensory input and brain predictions.

According to Barret, emotions are generated spontaneously and concurrently in multiple brain areas. Furthermore, emotions are unique to each individual. Our emotions are formed by combining unique sensory input and the brain's best predictions. According to the theory, the brain does not just create emotions based on the situation. Rather, the source of emotions is found in each individual's experiences. The brain predicts and anticipates sensory inputs like vision and taste. Sensory inputs either confirm the mind's predictions as correct or teach the brain to learn and correct incorrect predictions.

3) Our culture and beliefs shape our understanding of emotion.

Our reality is determined by the concepts we use to describe what we see around us, which are influenced by our culture. As a result, our understanding of what emotions are is a cultural convention. It means that once we understand the concept of emotion, we can experience it. For example, in the Tahitian language, there are no words for sadness. Rather, they use a phrase that means something along the lines of "flu fatigue."

Types of Emotions

All people experience eight fundamental emotions, regardless of background and culture. These eight basic emotions, each with its own unique and distinctive reactions and facial expressions, are joy, sadness, fear, disgust, surprise, anticipation, anger, and trust. There are eight basic emotions and many more variations of them.

Where Do These Eight Types of Emotions Come From?

The Plutchik Model, also known as the Feelings Wheel, was developed by psychologist Robert Plutchik. Plutchik wheel of emotions categorizes these eight basic emotions based on their physiological function. He created it to show the emotions and their possible combinations. He began with the premise that we have certain basic emotions that evolve and transform throughout our lives. People must adapt their way of being to the reality around them, and this interaction changes their way of feeling. Plutchik's Wheel highlights these changes to help us better understand them and have better emotional health.

The wheel resembles a multicolored flower. Each petal represents the progression of the basic emotions. There are eight petals and three main axes: typology, antagonism, and intensity.

The first is divided into two types of emotions: basic and composite. The basic ones are felt naturally, while the composite ones are a combination of the natural ones.

Antagonism, the second axis, refers to the opposition between the various emotions. In this case, we have four opposing emotions: joy/sorrow, anticipation/surprise, disgust/confidence, and fear/anger.

The third axis, intensity, reflects emotions and is represented by color. If emotion is very strong, it will be basic and close to the flower's center.

The Plutchik's Wheel and its Basic Emotions

Anger

Anger is a strong emotion characterized by feelings of agitation, hostility, antagonism, and frustration toward others. Anger, like fear, can cause the body to respond with a flight or fight response. A threat can elicit rage, prompting you to flee or fight to protect yourself. Anger is our way of reacting to an offence, especially if done on purpose.

Body language such as turning away from someone, facial expressions such as glaring or frowning, tone of voice such as yelling or speaking gruffly, a physiological response such as turning red or sweating, and aggression such as kicking, hitting, or throwing objects can all express anger.

On average, men are more outwardly aggressive than women, so it stands to reason that they are also angrier. Women, according to research, experience anger as frequently and intensely as men and are motivated by rage as often as men. One study, conducted by scientists at Southwest Missouri State University and involving around 200 men and women, found that women appeared to be better able to control immediate, impulsive responses to anger.

Surprise

This is our reaction when something unexpected occurs to us and is defined as a physiological startle response caused by unexpected events. It is the most fundamental neutral emotion that can be either negative or positive. Someone scaring you as you walk could be an unpleasant surprise. When you come home and find your friends gathered to celebrate your birthday that is an example of a pleasant surprise. Surprising facial expressions include widening the eyes, raising the brows, and opening the mouth. People also express surprise through physical reactions such as jumping up or jumping back and verbal responses such as gasping, screaming, and yelling.

Fear

Scientists define fear as an emotional reaction to an unexpected threat; it is an intense emotion essential for survival. When confronted with fear, people respond with either a fight or flight response; accelerated heart rates, tensed up muscles, and sharpened mind This reaction prepares the body to either flee from danger or fight the threat, thus ensuring that one is ready to deal with threats in a given environment. Attempts to escape or hide from threats, facial expressions such as pulling back the chin or widening the eyes, and physiological reactions such as increased heart rate are all expressions of fear.

Fear can disrupt brain processes that allow us to regulate emotions, think before acting, act ethically, and read nonverbal cues and other information presented to us. This disruption harms our thinking and decision-making, leaving us vulnerable to intense emotions and impulsive reactions. Consequently, a threat stimulus, such as the sight of a predator, elicits a fear response in the amygdala, which activates areas involved in motor function preparation for fight or flight.

Adrenaline or epinephrine is the fear hormone that travels through the bloodstream to all cells in the body and has a similar effect to sympathetic nerve action. It is responsible for the increased heart rate, increased rate of breathing, and the dilation of blood vessels to the lungs and muscles felt when a situation triggers fear.

As one of the most fundamental human emotions, fear is hardwired into the nervous system and operates instinctively. We are born with the survival instincts required to react with fear when we sense danger or feel unsafe.

People experience fear differently, and although everyone experiences some degree of fear, women may be more sensitive and expressive to and about objects that cause anxiety as an emotion. Because they are perceived and cultured as weaker, women are more likely to experience fear at the sight of minor things like insects or even a rat.

Licensed psychotherapist Dr. Michael Aaron also specifies three (3) most common types of fears that his clients struggle with:

- The fear of failure (atychiphobia).
- The fear of the unknown.

- The fear of emotions.

Researchers from Escape Games describe three (3) categories of fear: Rational, Primal, and Irrational Fear.

a) Rational Fear

Where there is a natural, imminent threat, rational fears arise. The fear of being stabbed is reasonable if someone brandishes a knife at you. The fear of death is logical.

b) Primal Fear

Primal fear is an innate fear hardwired into our brains. These are fears such as arachnophobia (fear of spiders) or ophidiophobia (fear of snakes).

c) Irrational Fear

Irrational fears do not make logical sense and can vary significantly between people. Half of your brain is terrified, while the other half is baffled.

1. What type of fear do you experience most as a woman?
2. Do you believe that women are more prone to express fear than men?

Disgust

Disgust is a primary emotion expressed in numerous ways, including turning away from repulsive things, facial expressions like curling the upper lip and wrinkling the nose, and physical reactions like retching or vomiting.

Disgust can result from numerous factors, including an unpleasant odour, sight, or taste. According to experts, disgust evolved as a reaction to harmful foods. When people taste or smell contaminated foods, they become appalled. Repulsion results from infection, poor hygiene, rot, blood, and death. There is also moral disgust when people observe others engaging in immoral, distasteful, or evil behaviour. Organizational relationships between bosses and employees can be repulsive to other employees.

Women are quicker to express disgust against poor hygiene scenarios that include body odour and unflushed toilets, animal contamination; out-of-date foods; and risky sexual behaviours. According to lead author Val Curtis, these scenarios elicit disgust due to an ancestral proclivity to avoid what we suspect will cause infection; therefore, women are more likely to express disgust.

The sensation that something is offensive, poisonous, or contaminated is a universal trigger for disgust. Women can be easily disgusted by things they see with the physical senses (sight, smell, touch, sound, and taste), people's actions and appearances, and even ideas.

Sadness

Sadness is an ephemeral emotional state depicted through common symptoms like grief, disappointment, disinterest, hopelessness, and a depressed mood. Sadness is an emotion that everyone feels; in some cases, people suffer from severe and prolonged bouts of sadness, which can progress to depression. It requires social support to manage.

We can express sadness in a variety of ways, including quietness, a low mood, withdrawal from others, lethargy, and crying. The severity and type of sadness can differ depending on the cause, and people cope with sadness differently. Despair can cause people to avoid others and even give them negative thoughts about their lives, leading to devastating actions.

Reflections

1. *According to your observations, what effects does sadness have on women?*
2. *What are the common triggers of sadness in women?*
3. *Other than the death of a loved one, on what occasions have the women in your life expressed sadness?*

Anticipation

The emotion of anticipation can majorly affect our expectations when facing an event or situation. It can either amplify our hopes or compound our worries, mainly because it arises from our past experiences or information related to the matter at hand. If we are eager for something to happen, then there will be definite optimism surrounding it, which will undoubtedly positively shape our expectations. We may begin to daydream of the wonderful outcome of whatever is about to take place, and these expectations may provide us with motivation and courage as we prepare for it. On the other hand, if we feel anxious anticipation, we might make assumptions based on fear and anxiety that only fill us with dread rather than hope. The concern can form negative expectations about how dire things might be, making us even more emotionally vulnerable toward the results. It's important to stay conscious when forming such expectations from anticipation so that they don't become too lofty or oppressive; maintaining realistic perspectives on events and situations help us remain levelheaded no matter what happens. In short, anticipation can influence our expectations immensely depending on how it colors our emotions and responses. Thus, learning how to interpret and manage its effects is important for navigating any situation successfully.

Joy

Joy is a feeling of great pleasure, excitement and triumph that often follows a significant accomplishment or experience. It's the very essence of being satisfied and content with oneself and one's environment - one's world within. Joy is accompanied by a natural process of release and celebration; it can be felt throughout the body, mind, and soul. Generally speaking, joy arises from experiences of connection to loved ones, successes in life achievements (or dreams fulfilled), or moments of synchronicity when all elements come together in an 'Ah-ha' moment. Taking the time to pause in moments of wonderment or blissful reflection is often experienced most profoundly. For example, if you're sitting outside on a sunny day gazing at the vast beauty of nature, breathe out in gratitude for this moment - feeling the warmth on your skin and cool breeze rippling through your hair, take pleasure in your surroundings. And when done regularly, we can permanently integrate more joy into our spirit.

Trust

Trust is an emotion that can be hard to define, yet each of us knows it when we experience it. At its core, trust is a feeling of security, a subjective position that allows us to believe there will be no harm or damage after taking action. We all make decisions based on trust in the situation and those involved. If we don't feel any sense of trust, it becomes much more difficult to make a positive decision about how to proceed.

To illustrate this concept, imagine buying a car from a dealer. Trusting that you are making the right purchase requires understanding the vehicle's condition, knowing the dealership's reputation, and feeling confident that what they are telling you is accurate to move forward. Without considering any of these points, you may find yourself in a situation where you trust the dealer enough to make a purchase.

In short, trust is an important factor when considering taking action- it dictates how safe and secure we feel about our decisions going forward.

Sub-groups of Emotions

You can combine fundamental emotions. As a result of such a combination, three subgroups of combined emotions are formed. The combination of emotions produces new emotions:

Primary Combined Emotions:

Anger + Anticipation = Aggression.
Confidence + Fear = Submissiveness.
Disgust + Anger = Contempt.
Fear + Surprise = Alarm.
Joy + anticipation = Optimism.
Joy + Trust = Love.

Sadness + Disgust = Remorse.
Surprise + sadness = Disappointment.

Secondary Combined Emotions:

Anger + Sadness = Envy.
Confidence + Anticipation = Fatalism.
Confidence + Surprise = Curiosity.
Disgust + Anticipation = Cynicism.
Fear + Sadness = Despair.
Joy + Anger = Pride.
Joy + Fear = Guilt.
Sadness + Anger = Envy.
Surprise + disgust = Disbelief.

As you can see, the various types of basic emotions and their possible combinations equate to the sum of those emotions Plutchik's wheel can help us understand our own and others' emotions.

Reflections

A survey was conducted by Ruben and Raquel Gur, a husband-and-wife team at the University of Pennsylvania School of Medicine, on whether gender emotion variances result from underlying differences in brain biology. Their study discovered that while the amygdala is the same size in men and women, a second region called the orbital frontal cortex, which controls aggressive impulses, is significantly larger in women. They hypothesized that this could explain why women appear to be better at controlling explosive outbursts.

1. Do you believe that the study's findings are valid concerning your life?

2. *Does the inherent ability of women to control explosive outbursts enable them to manage their emotions and become emotionally empowered effectively?*
3. *What is the advantage and disadvantage of this ability?*
4. *As a woman, how do you respond to surprises?*
5. *Do you believe that surprises act as motivating factors for productivity?*
6. *If someone acted in a way to elicit negative emotions towards you, then organized a surprise party to celebrate you, will the act make amends?*

Emotions Are Changeable

Whatever you think and feel will only last as long as you hold onto it. You can determine how long that will be. Believing that emotions are generally beneficial but can be altered when they become problematic may help us recover from emotional upset and avoid depression and anxiety. The ability to manage difficult emotions, known as "emotion regulation," has been linked to various positive outcomes, including improved mental health, moral decision-making, memory, and overall well-being. It is often very effective to use an emotion-management strategy known as "reappraisal," which involves reinterpreting an emotionally upsetting event in a more positive light. However, some of us believe we have no control over our emotions.

A recent study by University of Toronto researcher Brett Ford and her colleagues discovered that emotions could be changed and controlled, for example, by leveraging reappraisal. Over 200 ten to eighteen-year-olds were asked whether they thought emotions could be changed or were unchangeable and whether they used reappraisal or suppression to deal with difficult emotions. The researchers then used surveys and parent reports to assess their emotional well-being at the start of the study and 18 months later, youths who believed emotions could be controlled used reappraisal more frequently and were less depressed 18 months later than those who did not. Furthermore, they did not try to suppress their emotions as frequently as other young people.

Coping with Negative Emotions

Negative emotions are defined as any feeling that makes you unhappy. These emotions cause you to dislike yourself and others and lower your confidence, self-esteem, and overall life satisfaction. Negative emotions prevent us from thinking, acting rationally, and seeing situations objectively. When this happens, we tend to see and remember what we want to see.

Negative emotions are entirely natural. We cannot appreciate positive ones if they don't exist. Negative emotions, in particular, can assist you in recognizing threats and feeling prepared to deal with potential threats, as Zein, Wyatt, and Grezes state in their 2015 journal. At the same time, if you notice a consistent tendency toward one emotion, particularly a negative one, it's worth investigating why. Ignoring them will not make them vanish!

You may fall into a rumination spiral if you spend most of your time thinking about negative situations that may have caused them. According to new research by Michl et al. (2013b), the tendency to keep thinking about, replaying, or obsessing over negative emotional situations and experiences is known as rumination. The following are reasons for negative emotions.

1) Unsatisfied needs

It is normal to experience sadness, anger, loneliness, envy, and other distressing emotions when your needs are not met, whether physical, spiritual, social, emotional, social, psychological, etc., in nature.

2) Conflict in a relationship

Interpersonal relationship problems are a common source of negative emotions. Relationships with friends, family, coworkers or romantic partners can all face such difficulties.

3) Ineffective coping abilities

A lack of coping skills to deal with everyday stress can cause many distressing emotions. Poor coping skills frequently exacerbate the problem or introduce new issues into the situation.

Effective Ways to Help You Cope with Negative Emotions

1) Recognize Your Emotions.

Examine yourself and identify the situations causing stress and negative emotions. Examining the source of the emotion and your reaction can provide useful information. Triggering events, e.g., an overwhelming workload can result in negative emotions. How you interpret what happened can affect how you feel about an event and if it causes stress.

2) Get an Outlet.

You will need to find healthy outlets for dealing with these emotions as you make changes to reduce frustration. You can use the outlets we have outlined below.

- Exercising can provide an emotional lift and outlet for negative emotions.
- Meditation can assist you in finding some inner space to work with so that your emotions do not overwhelm you.
- Finding ways to have fun and add more laughter to your life can help you change your perspective and relieve stress.

3) Change the Aspects Within your Control.

After understanding your emotions better and what causes them, you can begin to address the issue. If you reduce or eliminate some of your stressors, you may experience fewer negative emotions. You could accomplish this in a variety of ways, including:

- Changing negative thought patterns through the cognitive restructuring process.
- Learning assertive communication techniques to help you manage relationship conflicts.
- Reducing job stress, often by delegating tasks, developing boundaries, and seeking assistance.

4) Accept and Acknowledge Your Emotions.

Accepting negative emotions is another effective way of dealing with difficult emotions. Acceptance entails admitting that we are afraid, angry, sad, or frustrated. Instead of avoiding or suppressing these emotions, you allow them to exist without dwelling on them. Bad feelings may be unavoidable from time to time. Therefore, you should brainstorm ways to make yourself feel better. Let the past go. Going over negative events always takes you out of the present moment and makes you feel bad.

There is a "positive" aspect regarding negative emotions (pretty confusing, it might seem!). Negative emotions, when handled correctly, can have proven benefits for our well-being. Here are some unusually positive aspects of negative emotions!

1. Jealousy motivates you to work harder.

Jealousy is not always bad. Most of the time, it's what psychologists call "benign envy." Benign envy has been shown to motivate students to perform better on tests and in schoolwork by making it more tangible for them to succeed (van de Ven et al., 2011).

2. Guilt aids in the modification of negative behavior.

Guilt is an extremely useful emotion. It's our moral compass, and when it goes off, it's a good indication that we've done or said something hurtful to someone we care about. It's similar to our internal system for punishing ourselves when we make mistakes.

3. Anxiety encourages novel approaches to problems and challenges.

When anxious, we will do anything to avoid feeling that way again. Anxiety is closely linked to our fight or flight response, allowing your body to generate energy quickly in preparation for action. Biswas-Diener and Kashdan state that when confronted with dangerous situations, anxiety takes over and motivates us to seek solutions quickly to avoid danger in their 2014 book "*The upside of your dark side: Why being your whole self—not just your "good" self—drives success and fulfilment.*"

4. Sadness can assist you in paying more attention to detail.

Forgas highlights in his 2014 article that positive emotions indicate that everything is fine in our immediate surroundings, and negative emotions indicate challenges or new stimuli that require our more focused attention. Sadness alerts us to the fact that something is wrong and asks us to consider why, what is causing it, and what we need to do to fix it.

A Real-Life Example of Coping with Negative Emotions

Susan David, the author of Emotional Agility, shared an intriguing story in her book. She began travelling the world to meet clients as her coaching consultancy grew in popularity. She was sitting in a fancy hotel room, admiring the view and enjoying the amazing room service, when she felt guilty. What was the issue? She felt bad about being away from her family.

"I've realized that my guilt can help me set priorities and, on occasion, realign my actions," David writes. "My guilt out of constantly being on the road makes me miss my children and family." "When I spend more time with them, it reminds me that my life is on the right track. My guilt is a blinking arrow pointing at my loved ones and the life I want to live."

The Pitfalls of Positive Emotions

Has anyone ever tried to cheer you up by telling you to "just think positive"? Or have you ever heard that if you 'just think positive,' you'll be able to overcome a stressful situation? Perhaps you've told yourself that to be successful; you should "just think positive." If that's the case, how did that go? Were you able to 'think positively in the face of sadness, worry, or distress? And did positive thinking produce the desired results? True, our positive fantasies and dreams about the future can sometimes help us explore different possibilities. Positive thinking can also lift our spirits, if only briefly. However, the idea that positive thinking alone can get you to your goals and achieve great success is a "myth." Our society's focus on the power of positive thinking has some major pitfalls, as we highlight below!

1. Believing that you must always think positively can lead to feelings of guilt or failure.

It is natural to experience a wide range of human emotions, from happiness and joy to anger and sadness. It's challenging to think positively always. However, if you believe you should, you are setting yourself up for disappointment, guilt, and failure if you cannot do so. Positive thinking will not bring your goals or desires to fruition. You must still set realistic goals, work within your means, take active steps toward change, and have the necessary knowledge, skills, and motivation.

2. Positive thinking can be used as a band-aid.

Positive thinking can be used as a band-aid to help people avoid the underlying issues in their lives. Positive thinking can temporarily make us feel better, but the band-aid eventually falls off or must be ripped off, leaving the problem behind.

3. Constantly embracing positive emotions can keep us from experiencing difficult emotions and missing out on opportunities for change.

Thinking positively and reaching for the silver lining script or putting on rose-coloured glasses not only distorts our ability to assess situations realistically but also encourages us to avoid or distract ourselves from dealing with negative consequences. That is not acceptable. To be happier, we must learn to manage our unhappiness when we face a setback or a total disaster. Sometimes we need to feel despair, anger or worry to help us notice the things in our lives that aren't working. Our emotions and difficult thoughts can point us in the right direction and serve as a catalyst for us to live a more full and meaningful life.

4. We are predisposed to overestimation.

It's known as the "optimism bias," which means that we are more likely to believe good things will happen to us more frequently than bad things will happen to other people. The bias influences the types of risks we take and our attitudes toward those risks; it also keeps us going when we should be changing our lives and possibly even bailing out of some situations.

How To Deal with These Pitfalls

1. Leverage mental contrasting!

Mental contrasting is thinking positively about the desired future while focusing on the obstacles ahead. Why is mental contrasting so effective? The technique enables us to change our behavior in subtle, unconscious ways that we are unaware of. Mental contrasting, in particular, creates strong mental links between the future and obstacles, as well as obstacles and the means to overcome them. It helps us recognize the obstacles in our path and energizes us. Finally, contrast allows us to see setbacks as valuable information that will help us achieve our goals. These nonconscious processes are triggered by mental contrast and predict the exerted behavior change.

Illustration of the Pitfall of Positive Thinking at Play

Per a recent Journal of Experimental Social Psychology publication, idealized thinking can sap motivation. Researchers asked college student volunteers to fantasize about a positive experience, e.g., topping an essay contest. They then assessed how the fantasy affected the subjects and what happened in reality. As measured by blood pressure, participants' energy levels plummeted when they imagined the most positive outcome. They reported having a worse experience with the actual event than those who imagined more realistic or negative outcomes.

The researchers compared lists of goals the subjects had set for themselves against their accomplishments to assess their real-life experiences. One of the study's co-authors at New York University, Heather Barry Kappes, believes that "When you fantasize about something very positive, it is almost like you're living it." "It tricks the mind into thinking you have attained your goal, removing the motivation and desire to 'get energized to achieve it,'" she explains.

When Is One Emotional?

According to the Collins dictionary, when a person uses feelings to think, act, and react to situations by expressing them very openly, primarily because they are upset; or when their state of mind is out of control by overly expressing joy or anger, they are said to be emotional.

Jaime Elmer, writing for Healthline, suggests that emotions are normal, but many people may wonder why they're feeling so emotional after an outburst or a crying session. These outbursts and uncontrolled expression of emotions form the state of being 'Emotional.' He adds that feeling heightened emotions or being unable to control your emotions can be caused by diet, genetics, or stress. It could also result from an underlying medical condition, such as depression or hormonal imbalances.

Highly emotional people are often profoundly compassionate and self-aware, but at the same time may feel exhausted from feeling such feelings all the time, according to Juliet V, author of the article 16 habits of highly emotional people. A highly sentimental person feels things more deeply and for a more extended period than the average person.

In an example, she gives us a glimpse of what she believes a highly emotional person portrays:

> *"Do you feel overwhelmed by your emotions when angry, sad, or embarrassed? Do you always cry during movies (especially when a character dies)? Do you go out of your way for friends and strangers alike because you want people to feel loved? Then you are an extremely emotional person."*

Unfortunately, when women express emotions like anger, crying because of sadness, or frustration, it is frequently pushed onto sentimental issues or deflected onto other people. An overwhelming circumstance or demand could lead to an emotional state, specifically through a feeling of frustration.

Reflections

You have three (3) back-to-back tests tomorrow and have not had time to study for any of them; you work two jobs, and your supervisors are on your neck about your lack of concentration and performance today.

1. *What emotions run through your mind as you read this?*
2. *What would you do in this situation?*
3. *Have you ever been branded emotional for expressing certain emotions?*
4. *On average, would you consider yourself an emotional person?*

Emotional Triggers

Simply put, triggers are automatic reactions to certain stimuli; they can be people, places, or things, and they can also be smells, words, or colors. Emotional triggers are automatic reactions to how others express their emotions, such as anger or sadness that always elicit an emotional response from us.

Emotional triggers represent the reaction to events based on one's surroundings and frame of mind, ranging from memories, experiences, or events that elicit an intense emotional response, regardless of one's current mood. Crystal Raypole explains in an article titled Coping in the Moment that emotional triggers spring from feelings of rejection, betrayal, unjust treatment, challenged beliefs, helplessness or loss of control, being excluded or ignored, disapproval or criticism, feeling unwanted or unneeded, feeling smothered or too needed, insecurity, loss of independence

Our thoughts, experiences, and memories are all linked to triggers. We connect a previous interaction with a similar emotional trigger and the current situation. When we don't understand why we react the way we do, we're more likely to blame the position or the person who caused the reaction.

How To Recognize Triggers

To recognize these triggers, pay close attention to your body and mind when situations generate a strong emotional response. There are both physical and emotional responses such as surging emotions and physical symptoms of anxiety such as a pounding heart, an upset stomach, shakiness or dizziness, or sweaty palms.

We must understand that thoughts always come before emotions arise.

- Our memories and past experiences influence our thoughts
- When we have similar emotional reactions to certain behaviors, like crying or anger, those behaviors may be triggers for our thoughts
- When we identify which thoughts trigger our emotional reactions, we can change them and choose a more helpful response

Reflections

1. What types of emotions do you encounter most in your daily life?
2. Do you believe that you are prone to more emotionally taxing or demanding situations as a woman?
3. List the types of emotions you encounter daily.
4. From the examples you listed in part four (4), which ones would you like to let go of and why?
5. What triggers the emotions that you encounter in your daily life?

How Do Our Emotions Affect Our Actions?

As Dr. Simon and others have pointed out, emotions influence, skew, or sometimes wholly determine the outcome of a large number of decisions that confront us within a day

Emotions can have a significant impact on thoughts and actions. The sentiments one experiences daily can compel one to act and influence the decisions one makes in life, both big and small. Even when one believes that their choices are logical and rational, emotions play a significant role.

Emotions serve various functions and can be fleeting, persistent, powerful, complex, and life-altering. They can inspire us to act in specific ways and provide us with the tools and resources we require to interact meaningfully in our social worlds.

Emotion significantly impacts human cognitive processes such as perception, attention, learning, memory, reasoning, and problem-solving. Feelings have a powerful influence on concentration, particularly in modulating attention selectivity and motivating action and behavior.

According to some theories linking emotion and behavior, emotions activate fixed behavioural "programs"; emotions like anger activate aggressive actions. Others argue that, while feelings do influence behavior, how they do so is determined by the individual's prior experiences and the current context.

> *When confronted with a bullying boss, your anger may prompt you to respond aggressively if this has worked for you in the past; alternatively, it may encourage you to go off and strengthen bonds with colleagues.*

In an example drawn from study.com to illustrate the effects of emotions on behavior;

Reflections

> *Joan is frustrated. She feels like her emotions go up and down. One minute she's very happy, but something happens that makes her angry or frustrated. She has noticed that the way she feels influences the way she acts. Sometimes when she's frustrated, she says and does things to her parents that she's not proud of doing.*
>
> 1. *Why do you think Joan is acting the way she does?*
> 2. *From the example, do emotions affect behavior?*
> 3. *What does Joan need to learn to salvage the situation with her parents?*

Motivation and emotion are very closely linked. Emotions like frustration and boredom can lower motivation and, thus, reduce the chance that we will act.

> Take Amanda, who has violin practice. If her teacher is too demanding or the piece she's practicing is too hard, she will feel frustrated and not interested in practicing. As a result, she might skip practice.

On the other hand, interest and enthusiasm are two emotions that can increase motivation, which increases the chance that we will act.

From the example, *assuming Amanda is supposed to practice a piano piece that she likes or is enthusiastic about playing, she'll be more likely to be motivated and, therefore, more likely to practice her piano.* Examples adapted from How Emotions Affect Behavior. (2016, June 28)

This observation is accurate concerning all humans, especially women. Looking at all the work we must do by the end of the day may lead to frustration and loss of motivation, anger, and all sorts of emotional reactions that will be all over the place, not forgetting hormonal changes and influences.

Emotions may spark a tendency to take specific actions to experience positive reactions and reduce the likelihood of experiencing negative emotions. *You might, for example, seek out social activities or hobbies from which you may derive a sense of happiness, contentment, and excitement. On the other hand, you would most likely avoid situations that could lead to boredom, sadness, or anxiety.*

In her article on *The Purpose of Emotions*, Kendra Cherry suggests that Emotions increase the likelihood that you will act. When you are angry, you are more likely to confront the source of your annoyance. When you are afraid, you are more likely to flee the threat. When you are in love, you may seek out a partner.

Reflections

When faced with a significant decision, do you go with your instinct or make a detailed list of pros and cons?

Following your intuition can help you get in touch with your true desires. Even if you believe your decisions are logical and based on common sense, they are frequently influenced by emotion. By understanding how emotions affect our decision-making, we can learn to strike the perfect balance between reason and intuition, allowing us to live the best life possible.

Therefore, emotional decision-making can influence the decision's outcome and speed; *Anger can cause impatience and hasty decisions. When you're excited, you might make snap decisions without thinking about the consequences while riding the wave of confidence and optimism about the future. When you are afraid, your choices may be clouded by uncertainty and caution, and you may take longer to decide.*

Advertisers also rely on the pester power to affect parent's emotions. It causes them to purchase products; as they display advertising that appeals to youngsters, who upset their parents, causing them to make purchasing decisions that may not be helpful or budgeted. Different emotions have different effects on judgments. When you're sad or irritated, you may be more willing to accept things that aren't in your best interests, such as not putting yourself forward for promotion or staying in an unhealthy relationship. But sadness can make you more generous; studies show that unhappy people are more likely to support increasing welfare benefits than angry people who lack empathy.

While intuitive decisions may be quick, especially in life-or-death situations where one does not have time to weigh the pros and cons of coffee or tea, instinctive reactions may be unfounded at times. However, they may also protect you from danger or prevent you from repeating past mistakes. This observation means that your instinct plays an essential role in decision-making, but it can also lead to poor judgment, unconscious bias, recklessness, or risk-aversion. So, are there ever times when we should listen to our gut feelings?

A 'bad feeling' in the pit of your stomach caused by a situation or person could be your body's way of warning you that it detects danger based on your previous experiences and beliefs. Some women have reported that they sensed something was wrong and later discovered something had happened to a loved one.

Emotions largely influence today's decisions. Your success may hinge on your ability to understand and interpret them because emotional responses by design appraise and summarize an experience that informs one's actions, thus influencing many decisions. However, emotions may bring devastating consequences if not mastered, mainly if negatively expressed.

The speed and utility of emotions compensate for their shortcomings in sophistication and precision. When emotions are not disordered, they provide information about some circumstances in a simple, quick manner that does not require much cognition. As a result, they communicate whether a situation is optimal or not aligned with a goal and how one might approach it.

Emotions play an adaptive role in that they prompt you to act quickly and take actions that increase your chances of survival and success. Fear can sometimes trigger the body's fight-or-flight response, which causes a series of physiological reactions that prepare the body to either stay and face the danger or flee to safety.

Charles Darwin proposed that emotional displays could also play a role in safety and survival. If you came across a hissing or spitting animal, it would be clear that the creature was angry and defensive, prompting you to back off and avoid potential danger.

Emotions can also get the body ready to act. The brain's amygdala (a cluster of almond-shaped cells located near the base of the brain), in particular, is in charge of eliciting emotional responses that prepare your body to deal with emotions such as fear and anger.

Emotions can assist a decision-maker in determining which aspects of a decision are most pertinent to their particular situation. They may also assist people in making faster decisions.

Reflections

Jannine is negotiating a contract when she becomes anxious; something doesn't feel right, and her emotional system alerts her to the need to assess the situation further. She can choose to allow her anxiety to disrupt her, or she could examine it. Under these circumstances, either:

1. *The other person reminded her emotional brain of someone who took advantage of her in the past.*
2. *This person did the same thing or portrayed a certain mannerism he has that elicited her anxiety*
3. *Her anxious reaction was a response to the other person or feedback to herself that she had a fear of success or failure?*

Case Study- Influence of Emotions on Behavior Influenced by Expectations

For the first experiment, the researchers informed volunteers that they would be completing a real negotiation task with financial ramifications as part of a study on peer influence. The dispute was over the distribution of colored chips. Each participant received a table with the monetary value of the chips, but they were also told that the values on the other person's table might not be the same.

Before the negotiation, the scientists assigned half of the participants to the "angry" condition. They read testimonials purporting to be from people who had previously succeeded at the negotiation task, with comments such as, "Throughout the negotiation, I was persistent." I eventually became enraged, and my partner felt compelled to give me what I desired." During the experiment, the scientists introduced a pilot study in which the participants also listened to "angry" music rated as inducing feelings of rage, such as Inquisition by the cello metal – yes, cello metal by the band Apocalyptica. The control group read testimonials that did not mention emotions but instead emphasized the importance of being "reasonable." They listened to music that was deemed emotionally neutral. Finally, the volunteers described their current emotional state before engaging in the negotiation.

The researchers found that the volunteers who said they felt angry made more money, but only if they'd read the testimonials advocating the benefits of anger, not if they hadn't. Those who'd read the emotionally neutral testimonials did equally well, whether they felt angry or not.

Male Emotions vs. Female Emotions

Psychologically, men and women appear to process and express emotions differently. Women, except for anger, experience emotions more intensely and share their feelings with others more openly.

Women are more likely than men to express their emotions verbally. Men are socialized from a young age to believe that expressing their sentiments is uncharacteristic of the male identity, as doing so may tarnish their image of being strong and stoic. Men, in particular, are told that crying in public will make them appear weak and jeopardize their masculinity.

As a result, men often find it difficult to express their emotions, even when intense; consequently, inadequate emotional communication can lead to frustration and tension in relationships. It can also be challenging for men to deal with emotions when communicating them to the opposite gender.

On the other hand, women are frequently taught that expressing their emotions is acceptable, even desirable. Women may be perceived as emotional or irrational, but it also allows women to have closer, more meaningful relationships with others.

The Male Emotions

Emotions associated with dominance or strength is perceived as more masculine, even if the underlying emotion fueling the behavior is different. But when men are conditioned to hide their emotions at all costs, those feelings have to find a way out. They usually compensate by behaving in a more stereotypically masculine manner.

Society, culture, and expectations teach men to hide their emotions, but that doesn't mean they don't have them. According to research, men experience emotions on the same level as women. However, because it is not socially acceptable for a man to cry when he is sad, it may appear that men do not experience sadness at all.

Being told to "man up" or "act like a man" is something that men learn as children and carry into adulthood. Over time, men become extremely adept at turning off their emotions or coping with them in ways more acceptable to males. It perpetuates a toxic masculinity cycle that can be difficult to break once it has become ingrained.

The Female Emotions

Women are more likely to express happiness, warmth, and fear, which aid social bonding and appear more consistent with the traditional role of primary caregiver. In contrast, men are more likely to express anger, pride, and contempt, consistent with a protector and provider role. Girls are expected to exhibit higher levels of most emotions in many Western cultures, particularly positive feelings like happiness and internalizing negative emotions like sadness, fear, anxiety, shame, and guilt. Girls are also expected to be more empathetic and sympathetic than boys.

Studies show that men and women more accurately display gender-stereotypic expressions, as men more accurately express anger, contempt, and happiness, while women express fear and contentment more accurately. When things go wrong, women tend to blame themselves rather than be objective about the various factors at work.

According to sociologists, culture and context-specific gender roles have a more substantial influence on emotional expression than biological factors. Empirical evidence suggests these factors socialize girls to be highly emotionally expressive, nonaggressive, nurturing, and obedient. In contrast, the same elements condition boys to be unemotional, aggressive, achievement-oriented, and self-reliant. Peers continue this process as children mature, constraining how, where, why, and with whom they express certain emotions.

Women are also perceived to possess an intuitive nature or a sixth sense that produces a gut feeling or perception. Though often ignored, it creates a certain kind of wisdom in women that men cannot understand; consequently, women can tell whether the business or investment decision a man is over the roof about will work or go down the drain. On the other hand, this 'gift,' if not mastered, can be disastrous.

Our ability to feel and process emotions is part of what makes us human. When we avoid those emotions, it can have several negative consequences. Suppressing emotions can lead to depression and anxiety, but it can also increase the risk of suicide in men.

Men and women need to remember that both genders have emotions that we must respect when working together. If you're a man working with a woman, it's imperative to be aware of how she expresses emotions and try to understand what she's feeling. If you're a woman working with a man, understanding that he may not be as open to His emotions as you may be is essential. Ultimately, it's critical to remember that we're all human with feelings. We should make an effort to be understanding of others, regardless of gender.

Why Do Our Emotions Hold Us Back?

Generally, emotions hold both men and women back. However, since women are stereotyped as the weaker gender, with more feeble emotional control, their emotions tend to cause an imbalance in reasoning and functioning, thus holding the woman back. When we allow people to study and exploit our emotions, convincing us to believe and accept things against our principles or better judgment, we inadequately react to certain stimuli, thus holding appropriate actions back.

Dawn Gregory, an emissary from A Universe Made of Love, refutes the concept that emotions can hold us back. He argues that the only way this is possible is because others use emotions to persuade us to believe things contrary to our better judgment, thus holding us back. When emotions enter the picture, people tend to believe whatever they hear. Sentiments are carefully cultivated to entice us to purchase whatever they aim at selling, but emotions are not the issue. Emotions are neither good nor bad; they simply exist. Emotions only hold us back if we let others manage them for us.

It is our resistance to emotions, as well as our desire for quick fixes, that makes them a problem. We want to feel "good" again when we think "bad." We believe in someone who promises to make us feel good. We later feel bad about ourselves because we feel misled.

Emotions are feelings that stem from our thoughts and can guide our actions. However, our emotions can sometimes hold us back from achieving our goals because our emotions can often be irrational and cloud our judgment.

Reflections
1. *Have emotions held you back in the past?*
2. *Do you feel that they did so because you are a woman?*

Which Emotions Are Holding Us Back?

There are a variety of emotions such as fear, anger, sadness, shame, and guilt that can hold us back from achieving success. These emotions can often prevent us from taking action or pursuing our goals. They can also cause us to feel overwhelmed and stressed. It is essential to understand and identify these emotions to learn to manage them effectively.

Not knowing whether to follow our instincts as women or the inability to master emotions and attain emotional maturity can also hold back women. Consequently, women suppress emotions because they believe they should or because feelings contradict who they think they are.

When we judge ourselves harshly, we invalidate our emotions and allow others to disapprove or not take our feelings seriously. Self-judgment inhibits your genuine sentiments, leading to numerous harmful effects for you and the people around you.

Dishonesty about our desires deters us from connecting with our actual sentiments. Refusing to let go of the past also holds us back. We always prefer to identify with our story that represents the past; being engrossed in the past deters you from current emotional experiences.

To break free, women must learn to manage their emotions and speak, or express themselves freely, voicing out what they feel, why they think it, and how important it is to them. Unapologetically speak out! We must also be honest and gentle with ourselves, knowing that we are enough. We must seek to let go of the past and remember that we can conquer practically anything by feeling our feelings and working through them. Be yourself, enjoy yourself, and stop being so hard on yourself.

Facts about Emotions

As discussed before, human biology includes emotions. They are chemicals that aid in regulating our minds and bodies, allowing us to make more informed decisions, interact with others, and navigate life. We experience emotions to help us pay attention, focus, and act. While they can be perplexing, emotions are a part of who we are, so we should learn how to use them effectively, and these nine essential facts about emotions are a good place to start!

1. Emotions are neutral.

There are no such things as positive or negative emotions. Emotions are simply a tool for communication and a way for our psyches to communicate with us. Our psyche may be communicating whether or not a need is being met or whether or not something is consistent with our values. The situation's outcome is determined by how we respond to the emotion.

For example, we may interpret that feeling negatively if we are jealous. However, the feeling may tell you that another person possesses the quality you want. At that point, you can react to the emotion with judgment or hostility toward yourself or the other person. Alternatively, you can channel your jealousy into action to meet that need within yourself.

If you need to assign value, your response determines whether the emotion is productive or unproductive. Nonetheless, the actual emotion is neutral. When people are happy, they feel expansive, and when angry, they feel contracted. So, if emotions are neutral, why do certain emotions, such as joy or love, feel so much better in our bodies? Because emotions have different weights, some are naturally heavier than others. It is critical to remember that this is still about density, not value. Dense emotions can be heavy or constricting, but that doesn't make them bad.

2. Emotions are contagious.

Even when we aren't paying attention to our emotions, they spread like viruses. We can "catch" negative and positive emotions in a group or with just one other person. The evolutionary explanation is straightforward: humans have only survived and thrived in groups. We are social beings. As a result, we are prone to picking up on each other's emotional states. If everyone around you is depressed, you will be depressed as well. When everyone is happy and excited, it spreads and makes others happy.

We constantly send and receive emotional messages via various mechanisms such as voice inflextion, facial expressions, posture, and specific behavioural patterns. It's a vital form of communication we all engage in, even if we don't realize it.

3. In about six seconds, emotions are absorbed in the body.

Each burst of emotional chemicals lasts about six seconds, from when it is produced in the hypothalamus to when it is completely broken down and absorbed. If we feel something for more than six seconds, we recreate and refuel those feelings on some level. If the tiger is chasing you, those fear chemicals are helping to save your life. Sometimes it isn't. However, emotional intelligence is about recognizing our emotions, evaluating their purpose concerning our circumstances, and deciding whether to recreate them.

4. Emotions are electrochemical signals that constantly pass through us.

They are released in our brains in response to our world perceptions. We feel them all the time. Emotions are constantly released in our brains and circulated throughout our bodies. They are also produced by our bodies and travel to our brains.

5. Emotions are physical.

It isn't easy to describe an emotion without mentioning how one's body feels or looks. Our physical, emotional, and mental states are all intertwined and affect one another. They are so closely related that they are practically interchangeable. According to a study conducted by a team of Finnish scientists, emotions are felt outside of the brain in the rest of the body and are a psychological phenomenon. During emotions such as love, happiness, and pride, certain parts of the body, particularly the upper half, are heavily stimulated, whereas depression and sadness are associated with numbness.

6. Colours can influence your emotions.

Colours and emotions are inextricably linked. Warm colours elicit different emotions than cool colours, and bright colours elicit different emotions than muted colours. It all depends on how colour's psychological effects are used. Colours may make us sad, happy, relaxed, and even hungry. These responses are influenced by psychological factors, biological conditioning, and cultural imprinting. It is crucial to understand the psychological effects of colours on the average person and the fundamentals of colour theory and colour meanings.

Warm colours are frequently associated with happiness and energy. Green, blue, and purple are examples of cool colours, which are soothing, but they can also express sadness. Yellow, orange, pink, and red are examples of happy colours. Pastel colours such as peach, light pink, and lilac can also improve your mood. Brighter and lighter colours will make you feel happier and more optimistic. Sad colours are dark and muted. Grey is the classic sad colour, but dark and muted cool colours such as black, blue, green, or neutrals such as brown or beige can have similar effects on emotions depending on how they are used.

7. All people are born with basic emotions (basic emotions are universal).

Paul Ekman identified six basic emotions (surprise, sadness, happiness, fear, disgust, and anger) in the twentieth century. Robert Plutchik identified eight, which he divided into four pairs of opposites (joy-sadness, anger-fear, trust-distrust, and surprise-anticipation).

According to popular belief, basic emotions evolved in response to the ecological challenges faced by our distant ancestors and are so primitive as to be "hardwired," with each basic emotion corresponding to a distinct and dedicated neurological circuit. Basic emotions are hardwired, innate and universal, automatic and fast, and trigger behaviour with a high survival value. Little can be said about more complex emotions like humility or nostalgia, which are never attributed to animals and infants.

University College London researchers led by Professor Sophie Scott investigated if the sounds associated with surprise, disgust, sadness, fear, anger, and happiness are shared across cultures. The University of London study compared people from the United Kingdom and Namibia. According to the findings, basic emotions like sadness, fear, anger, and amusement are shared by all humans.

8. You can cultivate and change your emotions.

Due to the amazing prefrontal cortex, you can shift your attention away from emotion, interpret it differently, or even change its meaning and, thus, your reaction. Fear, anger, sadness, anxiety, worry, shame, and guilt are all powerful emotions that can negatively impact our well-being. Negative states and moods are created when our disempowering emotions linger for an extended period; being mindful and aware of our feelings aids in releasing negative emotions. The intensity of the negative emotion is reduced when the emotion is pinpointed. It moves us from the actor position, where we feel it, to the observer position, where we notice it.

When we name something, we draw our attention and consciousness to it rather than allowing it to affect us unconsciously in the background. This way, we can easily cultivate positive emotions, such as happiness, while eliminating negative ones, such as sadness.

9. What you eat and drink may affect your emotions.

Did you know that the foods you eat can influence how you feel? Poor food choices can cause energy slumps, low mood, and difficulty sleeping. As a result, it is critical to consume more foods that promote positive emotions, such as protein. Consuming foods rich in protein is necessary for a good mood. Amino acids can be found in fish, red meat, poultry, eggs, and legumes. Tryptophan is an essential amino acid that aids in the production of serotonin in the brain. Serotonin is the "happy hormone" because it promotes calm and relaxation while protecting against depression. Carbohydrates are also necessary. Our brain is primarily powered by glucose, which we obtain from carbohydrate-rich foods. Severe carbohydrate restriction can make you grumpy and tired because the brain no longer receives an adequate glucose supply.

Final Thoughts

So, what have we learned about emotions? We know that they are important for our survival and well-being, that they are formed in response to stimuli, and that they affect our actions. We've also looked at the different types of emotions and how men and women experience them differently. With this understanding of emotions, let's explore ways to cope with difficult emotions and become emotionally mature.

CHAPTER 2:

WOMEN AND THEIR EMOTIONS

In this chapter, we'll explore the role of emotions in women's lives and why they should be embraced, not feared. We'll also discuss how to manage difficult emotions and use them to your advantage. We will also look at emotional baggage that women sometimes have. Embrace your emotions - they make you unique and powerful!

Women As Emotional Beings

Women encounter many situations and responsibilities that expose them to many emotional triggers. Different circumstances have resulted in a breakdown, particularly for the modern or present-day woman who must balance her inherent feminine roles' social demands, and career. The most common roles women have and experience emotions are:

Motherhood and Parenting

Women go through intense emotions on their motherhood journey, some of which saturates the senses. Many of these emotions cause a mother to stumble, while others assist her in thriving. Motherhood is said to be a divine emotion, an unrivalled sensation that creates the most beautiful and strongest bond with your child. It makes a mother the happiest person on the planet. This is because many women enjoy the emotions triggered by holding, touching, observing, smelling, and playing with their children, especially in the early stages of motherhood. However, some mothers may not experience the overwhelming sense of love they were hoping for right away.

Motherhood demands a lot from women bringing a variety of roles as a nurturer, storyteller, comforter, supporter, problem solver, and others. Despite the joys that motherhood brings, it causes feelings of loss, fear, worry, guilt, pain, pride, disappointment, and frustration.

Reflections

1. *Have you experienced motherhood?*
2. *What are the joys and pains you have encountered in this journey?*
3. *Do you believe that the emotional distress of motherhood is worth it? Why?*
4. *Knowing what you know about motherhood, would you like to share in the experience one day?*
5. *How do you think motherhood will change your life, emotional experiences, and emotional expressions?*

Singlehood

According to sociologists' celibacy refers to a choice made by individuals who choose not to enter into a relationship based on their preferences or previous relationship experiences. As a result of this modern trend, individuals have chosen to have children without partners and own property or live alone without a partner.

The relationship between women's emotions, life satisfaction, and singleness is bidirectional: Negative emotions and low life satisfaction would be triggered by involuntary singlehood and this leads to loneliness, sadness and anger. However, the feelings experienced by single women can vary greatly and often depend on the individual woman's life experiences. If a woman has chosen to be single, she will experience joy, peace and happiness from the freedom of doing whatever she pleases to do.

Loneliness is a prevalent emotion for single women and often occurs because they lack the support of a partner or spouse. Additionally, single women may feel isolated from their friends and family members in relationships. Sadness is another emotion associated with single women. It can be due to several factors, including the end of a relationship, not being able to find a partner, or feeling like they are not good enough.

Single women also experience anger that results from frustrations and feelings that arise from the perceptions of unfair treatment, such as in the workplace or in relationships. Additionally, single women may feel anger towards society for its expectations of them. Depending on several factors, the single woman may also experience happiness. This feeling may arise from enjoying their independence, a successful career, having supportive friends and family, or emotional relief from a taxing relationship.

Single women find it tough to manage society's expectations of them. As a single woman, one experiences varying emotions that can be difficult to manage and comprehend, especially if they are new to you. It is critical to have a support system when dealing with these emotions, whether friends, family, or a therapist. Talking about how you're feeling with someone can help you understand and manage your feelings healthily.

Reflections

1. *Are you a single woman?*
2. *What are the joys and pains you have encountered in this journey?*
3. *How do you think singlehood has changed your life, emotional experiences, and emotional expressions? In which ways?*

Married Life

Marriage is the most critical area in a woman's life where emotions take control; therefore, the feelings that married women frequently experience vary according to the individual. Marriage is a relationship that can breed the greatest fulfilment, apathy, or pain, depending on several factors.

Married women may experience happiness, love, contentment, and fulfilment. These feelings can be gratifying and strengthen the marriage. Furthermore, married women frequently experience a sense of security and stability within their relationship that proves highly beneficial, especially during difficult times. While all marriages have ups and downs, the emotions that married women commonly experience can help to strengthen the relationship.

A woman is naturally more emotionally connected, and her unhappiness in marriage is most likely due to a deep sense of unfulfilment. There is a sense that there is insufficient love, affection, trust, respect, or other essential components for a satisfying connection.

Lack of effective communication, ignoring boundaries, emotional or sexual infidelity, selfishness, value differences, and different life stages can all lead to marital breakdown if left unchecked.

Many married women enjoy marital bliss or the benefits and fulfilment of marriage and the parental joy that comes with it. However, without proper boundaries and awareness, feelings can lead to devastating expressions and unhappy endings, causing sadness, bitterness, anger, and even depression.

Reflections

1. *Are you married?*
2. *What are the joys and pains you have encountered in this journey?*
3. *Knowing what you know about marriage, what tips would you give to a single lady in terms of emotional preparedness?*
4. *How do you think marriage has changed your life, emotional experiences, and emotional expressions?*

Dealing With the Death of a Loved One

When dealing with the loss of a loved one (depending on who it is), women experience a wide range of mixed emotions that can be overwhelming as they progress through the emotional stages of grief: shock or disbelief, denial, bargaining, guilt, anger, depression, and acceptance/hope.

In this regard, the contrast with women is stark. Women frequently cry and talk openly about their pain. A man may appear cold, irritable, angry, or depressed, and he may find it difficult to express his pain. Women confide in their friends, express their feelings and emotions outwardly, and "feel" their way through grief.

Divorce or Separation

Life after divorce is fraught with conflicting emotions filling many women with rage, fear, resentment, and bewilderment. They may even feel ashamed or guilty, even if they do not deserve it. However, a 2013 study conducted by Kingston University researchers reveals that most women were significantly happier than they'd ever been after divorce. These findings may be factual, mainly if the marital relationship exhibited violence, abuse, feelings of rage, resentment, bitterness, frustrations, and the unwillingness to work things out. Consequently, the woman may find an emotional balance during the healing period and is now in more control of her emotions.

Reflection
1. *If you are divorced, what would you advise to someone thinking of going through it- in terms of emotional preparation?*
2. *How do you think divorce has changed your life, emotional experiences, and emotional expressions?*

Abuse: Physical, Emotional, Sexual

Abusive relationships or situations catch many women off guard. Women experience some form of abuse (emotional, physical, or sexual) throughout their lives, from childhood to adulthood. Most women do not detect the abuse until it is too late and difficult to let go.

Abusive relationships or situations may exist in a woman's daily life and may originate with her parents, siblings, children, work, or colleagues: friends or a romantic partner.

Emotional abuse is the most difficult to detect because it involves attempts to scare, control, or isolate a person in any relationship. Women must eliminate situations in their lives that cause the state of vulnerability to toxic friends, workmates, and family by being aware of and setting healthy boundaries to escape any form of abuse.

Hormonal Changes and Menopause

Dealing with hormonal changes, pre, and post-menstrual ovulation changes, and menopause in older women brings challenges. It requires a considerable level of maturity to remain emotionally stable.

When estrogen levels fluctuate, people, particularly women, who are more sensitive to hormonal change are more likely to experience depression, anxiety, mood swings, and other emotional symptoms.

According to the American College of Obstetricians and Gynecologists, "the constant change in hormone levels during this time can have a troubling effect on emotions... leaving some women feeling irritable and even depressed."

Hormones influence many emotions that people, especially women, experience daily Hormone levels that shift, fluctuate, or simply go haywire can seriously disrupt your feelings.

Reflections

1. *Have you experienced abuse or hormonal changes in your life?*
2. *How do you think these experiences have changed your emotions and emotional expressions?*

Emotional Baggage

Many women believe that when they sacrifice for the family, children, work, or parents, they will receive a miraculous reward for sacrificing themselves. When this is not forthcoming, they become disappointed and angry at everyone, including the whole world, branding them as ungrateful, unnoticing, and selfish.

With this comes the consequence of carrying emotional baggage dubbed 'the emotional backpack' that results from holding on to pain and disappointment, and unnecessary worry.

Karol Ward, in the article *Better by Today* by the NBC news titled "Is your emotional baggage holding you back? describes the proverbial backpack and how can we prevent it from filling up to the point where we feel like we can't carry all of our "stuff?" When discussing conflict, we continually stuff the burdens on our backs until one day, they can't zip, and the stuff starts spilling out all over the place."

Mental baggage: A coping mechanism;

"Emotional baggage or emotional backpacks describe all of the unresolved emotional issues; traumas and stresses from the past and present that occupy the mind and even body," says Karol Ward, LCSW, author of "Worried Sick: Break Free from Chronic Worry to Achieve Mental & Physical Health." "Mental baggage tends to ruminate or think negatively about unresolved past or current issues. Emotional baggage does feel like you are wearing or carrying a bag filled with emotions."

The Problem with Carrying a Heavy Load.

While carrying past experiences and the emotions that came with them may help us better navigate future experiences, they also take a toll on our health.

They say, *'do not wrong a woman because she will never forget!'* Have you ever been in a conflict with a loved one, especially of the opposite sex, and you remind them that this is not the first time they were doing this to you, and they go like, *"WHEN? LAST YEAR!" you stand there thinking the nerve! He even forgot!"*

A study conducted by three (3) researchers of the Norwegian Healthy Life Centre found that emotional baggage can be a barrier to making healthy lifestyle changes like exercising more, eating healthier, or quitting smoking. "Participants ascribed being burdened by an emotional baggage to problems from childhood or with family, work and social life issues." Respondents said they felt that emotional baggage was an essential explanation for why they were stuck in old habits. Conversely, being stuck in old habits added load to their already emotional baggage and made it heavier."

This baggage can also "interfere with professional ambition or goals, healthy relationships, personal contentment, and the enjoyment of life," says Ward. "Until you realize why your life is not going the way you want, you can feel like a victim, someone who is being tossed around by life's circumstances."

Reflections

1. *Have you fallen victim to any of these perception misconceptions?*
2. *Which emotional sacrifices have you made in the past?*
3. *What would you change about your perception as a woman to be in more control of your emotions?*
4. *Are you carrying an emotional backpack?*

Past emotional experiences will influence the interpretation and perception of current interactions and primary relationships. We often use negatively or positively prejudiced emotional responses that result from past experiences in our relationships. We limit ourselves when we suppress our emotions because we believe we should or because they contradict who we think we're.

Bottling up emotions normally entails suppressing the most profound feelings. It occurs when one avoids expressing how they truly feel, or prefer to keep their emotions to themselves. There is a fear that one will appear weak. Ignoring feelings puts one at risk of missing out on important information or being manipulated. *Acknowledge the emotion as it arises and allow it to pass. There is no "issue" that needs to be "resolved." The sentiment is not a problem in and of itself.*

However, the sentiment indicates that the emotion's situation may be a problem. You can be more objective in your conclusions about what is going on if you recognize the reaction and allow it to pass. There are no issues when we manage our own emotions.

Reflections

1. *Are there emotions that you need to acknowledge?*
2. *What is the primary reason why you are holding on to the feelings?*
3. *Are you ready to let go of these emotions for your empowerment?*

Final Take Away

At the end of the day, women are emotional creatures. We feel more deeply than men, and we process our emotions differently. This isn't a bad thing; it's just the way that we are wired. We must embrace our emotions and understand how they work to better deal with them. When it comes to loss, whether it is the death of a loved one or another type of loss, we need to allow ourselves to mourn in our way and give ourselves time to heal. The hormonal changes associated with menopause can also lead to increased feelings of sadness and anxiety, so it is important for us to be aware of these changes and take steps to manage our mental health during this time. Finally, we all have emotional baggage from our past experiences. It is important for us not to bury these feelings but rather acknowledge them and work through them to move on with our lives. By understanding how women's emotions work, we can learn to cope with them more healthily and ultimately become emotionally empowered women!

CHAPTER 3:

THE EMOTIONAL WOMAN STIGMA

There's a stigma against women that are seen as "emotional." Society tells us that we must be strong, independent and emotionless in order to be successful. This isn't fair to us or the people around us. We need to break free from this taboo and embrace our emotions. Only then can we truly be happy and fulfilled. Keep reading to find out how.

What Emotional Stigmas Do Women Face?

Women shoulder a lot and go through so many painful experiences brought about by our anatomy; furthermore, society expects much more from women than their male counterparts, leading to increased emotional stigma. Moreover, society perceives women as weak and incapable of dealing with difficult situations, a view frequently used to justify gender discrimination or violence against women.

One of the most common emotional stereotypes of women is that they are overly emotional or dramatic. This perception isn't always accurate, but society frequently portrays women as excessively sensitive beings who cannot control their emotions. Consequently, this significant issue often leads to the dismissal of women when they express their sentiments.

The society also expects all women to be caregivers and nurturers, adding another emotional stigma. Consequently, childless or single women feel strained, especially if they don't want to play this role. These expectations also demand that women take care of everyone else's emotions, but they are not permitted to have their own.

Happiness, sadness, love, anger, and fear are the most commonly associated emotions with women. When women display these emotions, they are considered "weak," but this isn't always the case. Women, like everyone else, experience a variety of emotions; the important thing is to learn how to control and use them advantageously instead.

Female hormones bring about many confusing psychological and physiological changes ranging from painful pre-menses experiences to managing the monthly period and ovulation phase, childbirth, carrying a child for nine (9) months, managing heartbreak and abuse, and finally handling and managing menopause. This combination/compilation should make women realize that they are vital if they can shoulder all these and remain sane.

We need to break free from several emotional stigmas about women. Some of these include the idea that women are emotionally unstable, that we are not as capable as men, and that we cannot handle stress or difficult situations. These stigmas can hold us back from reaching our full potential and being our best selves.

Picking up on emotions is essential, but you must also be able to overcome the stereotype of being an emotional woman. Women are conditioned to believe that crying isn't acceptable. Women are never sick or tired and must always be tough. Women often feel guilty about their loving nature and end up being something they are not just to "fit in" or make other people happy. Women always deal with opinions that make them feel like they are overreacting, overthinking, and overemotional

Why do we, as loving people, feel guilty about our loving nature? Why do we have to be "tough?" I'm tired of ladies trying to be someone they're not; I'm tired of hearing that. Why do we let others decide how much reaction, thinking, and emotion we allow ourselves to experience and display?

In response to the emotional woman stigma, Joyce Santos states:" *We are strong, powerful, and independent women simply because we love harder and deeper than others. Yes, we cry at a cheesy love tale, and yes, we need solid and emotional dialogues. Emotional women are the ones who make a difference in the world. Empathetic ladies are the ones that fly around the world to assist strangers in need. We may cry at every step of the road, but it's not because we're broken."*

Breaking Free from the Emotional Woman Stigma

There is a growing movement of emotionally empowered women breaking free from these stigmas and embracing their emotions. Emotionally empowered women are strong, capable individuals who understand the importance of taking care of themselves emotionally. They know how to manage their feelings and use them to their advantage.

Fortunately, a growing movement of emotionally empowered women is working to change the conversation about women and emotions, thus helping women overcome the harmful emotional stigma. Emotionally empowered women have learned to understand and manage their emotions healthily. They are not afraid of their feelings and do not allow them to hold them back.

Women can break free from emotional stigmas by learning how to manage their emotions effectively by understanding why we feel the way we do and taking steps to manage our feelings healthily. It also requires breaking the taboo around talking about our feelings and seeking out support when we need it. Emotionally empowered women are more successful, happy, and balanced. They understand their worth and value themselves highly. If you want to become more emotionally empowered, start by taking care of yourself emotionally. Women could make time for self-care, set boundaries, and communicate their needs regularly. It would help if you also learned how to embrace your emotions and use them advantageously. Women must also realize that emotional intelligence is key to mastering their emotions. Knowing how to manage your feelings enables you to achieve anything you set on your mind.

However, by becoming emotionally empowered, we can break free from the emotional woman stigma and instead embrace our emotions as a source of strength. When we are emotionally empowered, we can manage our emotions to allow us to stay balanced and healthy both mentally and emotionally.

Reflections
1. *Which of the two (2) stigmas have you personally experienced?*
2. *How did you overcome the stigma?*
3. *How can women overcome the harmful stigma of the emotional woman?*

Final Take Away

So what can we do to break free from the emotional woman stigma? We need to start by recognizing that these labels are harmful and work to dismantle them. We should also be mindful of our biases and how we might contribute to the problem. Finally, it's important to celebrate all aspects of femininity, including the emotional ones. Let's encourage girls and women to express their emotions freely, without judgement or shame. Working together can create a world where all women feel seen, heard, and loved for who they are.

CHAPTER 4:

HOW BELIEFS AFFECT OUR EMOTIONS

Have you ever wondered why you feel a certain way and can't seem to shake it? Well, your beliefs might be to blame! Believe it or not, our beliefs play a big role in how we feel emotionally. In this chapter, we'll explore how our beliefs can shape our emotions and how we can use them to be a more emotionally empowered woman for a happier life!

Our Beliefs Play a Huge Role

Our beliefs play an enormous role in shaping our emotions, our self-image, and our view of the world. Beliefs are powerful — they are the lenses through which we interpret life's experiences and form judgments about ourselves and others. Even subtle differences in belief can profoundly shape both our thoughts and behaviours. For example, if we believe that success is achieved primarily through hard work, we may experience a sense of pride after a challenging project is completed. However, if we believe that luck is a major factor in achieving success, we can feel discouraged when faced with failure.

Our beliefs also inform our self-image; if we believe that intelligence is determined by genetics, then we might give up when facing challenges because it feels out of our control to change. Conversely, believing that intelligence can be gained through effort can help us persevere in difficult situations.

As these examples demonstrate, being aware of how our beliefs affect our emotions can be empowering — when we recognize the links between what we think and how we feel, it gives us more control over how we choose to respond to whatever life throws at us. Understanding this connection between beliefs and emotions can help us carve out healthier pathways for growth and self-improvement.

Reflections
1. *How have beliefs affected your emotions and feelings towards a person, place or situation?*
2. *Identify 3 unhelpful or unhealthy beliefs you have towards something or someone?*

Be Aware of Your Own Personal Beliefs and How They Affect You

It's critical to be aware of our beliefs, as they can strongly influence how we feel about something or someone. Our experiences shape our values and opinions, and it's not uncommon for us to form rigid ideas without proper consideration. This can lead to strong emotional reactions that don't take into account different perspectives or audiences.

For example, suppose a person has a negative experience with an organization or person associated with their religion. In that case, they may develop a bias that colours their opinion of all instances related to that faith. Instead of using logic or facts to inform their decision-making, the pre-conceived beliefs might direct them toward specific conclusions regardless of whether there is evidence to support them. It's important to recognize the power of our pre-existing beliefs and ensure we are actively questioning them to make decisions based on more than just emotion. By taking the time to be mindful of our biases and beliefs, we can be better equipped for more objective decision-making in the future.

Reflections

1. *Identify 3 unhelpful or unhealthy beliefs you have towards something or someone?*

Beliefs about Beauty, Relationships, Motherhood, and Work

Our culture has a set of beliefs about beauty, relationships, motherhood, and work that are deeply engrained in our idea of success. These beliefs offer us a sense of belonging, validation, or peace of mind to carry out daily tasks and make decisions. When we feel that we can fit into these definitions of success, it offers us a sense of self-confidence and pride. However, when we don't feel like we measure up to society's standards, it can cause feelings of shame and guilt.

Beauty ideals have been particularly damaging for women with their unrealistic models and expectations about weight, body shape, and youthfulness.

Similarly, the pressure to find a significant other at just the right time or be the perfect mother can be extremely intimidating - not to mention the perpetuation of traditional gender roles in relationships and careers that make it difficult for many men and women to reach their true potential.

Acknowledging our beliefs about beauty, relationships, motherhood, and work is part of human nature - but they should never hold us back from being our true selves. As Mark Twain said, *"Whenever you find yourself on the side of the majority - it's time to pause and reflect."* Here's hoping that taking a moment to consider our beliefs and how they make us feel gives us room to grow without the strict parameters given by society.

After all - finding balance in life is far better than striving for perfection! Be brave enough to follow your heart!

Reflections

1. *Are you living authentically as yourself despite the challenges of conventional thinking?*
2. *Identify 3 ways that society's standards on beauty, relationships and motherhood have affected your life.*

We Must Question Our Beliefs

How does our inner life shape how we experience the world? Our thoughts, beliefs, and emotions all influence the way we perceive reality. That's why it's important to be mindful of what we tell ourselves on a daily basis. The beliefs that make up our personal philosophy about life and our place within it have a powerful impact on how we feel emotionally. A positive perspective can lead to greater emotional stability and resilience, while negative thinking can create feelings of stress, inadequacy, or despair. Being aware of what you believe can help you monitor its effect on your day-to-day life.

Upholding values that lead to emotional well-being—such as self-compassion, gratitude, and kindness— may help foster feelings of joy and contentment in your day-to-day existence. By actively questioning your beliefs and subsequent feelings, you can become more intentional about replacing toxic musings with more hope-filled ones. So don't forget that your beliefs play a crucial role in defining your emotional landscape. Practicing mindfulness in this regard is vital if you want to support your ongoing mental health journey.

Reflections

1. *What emotions do you feel when you consider beliefs about yourself? Are they positive or negative?*
2. *If negative, what new empowering belief can you adopt today about yourself?*

How To Change Negative Beliefs

Many of us have beliefs that we carry around that don't make us feel particularly empowered or capable. Maybe it's something from our childhood, like believing that we aren't good at math, or maybe it's something more recent, like feeling afraid to start a new business for fear of failure. Changing these beliefs isn't easy, but it can be done with a bit of determination and self-reflection.

One way is to really examine why you believe in the first place - if the reasoning behind your belief isn't sound, then there's no need to hold on to it. Also, challenge your perspectives by looking for evidence that disproves your limiting beliefs; this can help you evaluate the reality behind what you are telling yourself and allow you to create new thought patterns.

For example, if you have a hard time believing that you can be successful in a certain field, try finding stories of people who faced similar adversity and overcame it to achieve their goals - this will give you inspiration and confidence that you, too, can achieve great things!

Finally, practice positive affirmations; repeating empowering mantras out loud can help change how your mind perceives your abilities. With a little bit of effort and self-love, anyone can learn how to break down destructive thought patterns and create new beliefs that make them feel strong and capable.

Final Take Away

We all have beliefs that drive our emotions one way or another. It's vital to be aware of them so that we can question and change the ones that don't empower us. There are a few ways to go about changing these beliefs, but it starts with acknowledging their impact on our lives and feelings. Evaluate your beliefs for a more empowered life.

CHAPTER 5:

THE INFLUENCE OF CULTURE ON OUR EMOTIONS

In this chapter, each culture's unique set of values and beliefs has a profound impact on the emotions we feel. In this chapter, we'll take a closer look at the influence of culture on our emotions as women. We'll also explore how different cultures impact everything from our self-image to our relationships and why we feel the way we do.

How Different Cultures Affect Emotions

Culture gives structure, expectations, guidelines, and ground rules that help us understand and interpret emotions. For example, most Asian cultures prioritize social harmony over individual gain, while Westerner cultures originating from Europe and the United States prioritize individual self-promotion. Research indicates that individuals from the US are more likely to express negative emotions like anger, fear, and disgust when alone and with others. On the other hand, Japanese people are more likely to express the same feelings while alone.

In the Utku Eskimo population, there was a rare expression of anger, and when it did occur, it resulted in social ostracism. The cultural expectations of emotions are also known as display rules.

Psychologists (Ekman & Friesen, 1969; Izard, 1980; Sarni, 1999) believe people learn these rules during socialization. Friesen and Ekman (1975) also suggest that people can express these "unwritten codes" to guide emotions and internalize different rules as a function of an individual's gender, culture, or family background. Miyamoto & Ryff (2011) use cultural scripts to refer to cultural norms influencing how people expect emotions to be regulated. Cultural scripts determine how positive and negative emotions are experienced and combined. These scripts can also dictate how people regulate their emotions which later influence an individual's emotional experience. For instance, in Western cultures, the dominant social script maximizes positive emotions and minimizes negative emotions.

On the other hand, in Eastern cultures, the dominant cultural script focuses on "dialectical thinking" and efforts to strike a balance between positive and negative emotions. As a result of normative behaviours in these two cultures varying, we should expect their cultural scripts to also vary.

Tsai et al. (2007) argue that not only do cultural factors influence ideal effect (i.e., the affective states that people ideally want to feel) but that we can detect the influence very early. Their research suggests preschool-aged children are socialized to learn ideal effects through cultural products such as children's storybooks. This finding is consistent with American best sellers containing more exciting and arousing content in their books than Taiwanese best sellers. The findings show that cultural differences in which emotions are desirable or ideal become evident very early.

Why Are Emotions Cultural Phenomena?

From Psychology Today, the pioneer in cultural psychology, Baja Mesquita, reveals that emotions are a cultural phenomenon because we learn to have emotions culturally. When interacting with others, we learn to categorize and experience emotions in certain ways. In Western cultures, shame is often associated with destructive behaviours in the relationship: We withdraw in shame and do not want to show ourselves.

However, countries like India, Turkey and Pakistan, which have the Islamic culture, consider shame a good emotion and place it in one category with modesty and embarrassment- feelings that show that you have decency and that you occupy your rightful place in the world. Here is an example of an Islamic culture story that shows how the emotion of shame influences their culture:

Regarding modesty and shame, they are important Islamic ethics and morality. 1438 years ago, Prophet Muhammad said that, "Among the sacraments given to early prophets – which should reach the people -include the statement that; if you experience shame, then you can do whatever you wish." This statement meant that the earliest form of communication from the creator of the universe to individuals that were supposed to become prophets consisted of the demand for them to cease any shameful conduct. The shameful acts could question their humanity, moral rectitude and anything of value required for them to be commissioned into the prophethood. Therefore, in the Islamic culture, a person ordained as a prophet should not be a thief, a liar, a smug or a scoundrel. For a person to be a follower of a prophet or even a prophet of the almighty, they should be modest in conduct and speech."

The Islamic culture teaches that the first thing a nation must lose before its perdition is a sense of shame. For example, if a woman throws her modesty away, society will be on the verge of liquidation.

Christianity teaches us that our emotions are a reflection or expression of our soul. Inherently it reveals our values and desires that are interpreted as our emotions. The Bible often refers to various types of emotions; joy, love fear, anger and peace. But one of the pertinent things said on emotions is around exercising self-control, this is considered as the fruit of the Spirit (Galatians 5:23). Overall the Bible tells us to express our emotions and bring them to God who allows His peace to fill and guide us.

Therefore, from the description above, different cultures value the same emotion differently. The emotion is similar but has different consequences for relationships and behaviour. How you deal with shame, whether you reach out or withdraw, and the impact on your reputation and relationships are all cultural specifics.

Culture Influences Emotions

Universally the sauce of emotions is the interaction with other people which within the framework of culture. However, from there on, things are different between cultures. Nearly everything that relates to emotions is cultural. People learn emotions from observation and how people respond to them in the presence of certain emotions. Usually, we learned prescriptive norms, which include the rules that govern when to have different emotions.

For example, orthodox Islamic cultures regard divorce as "an act that God most despises" and consider it more traumatic than death. Additionally, how different cultures display grief varies even greatly across different cultures. Besides cultural variation in funeral burial rituals, whether the emotional display of grief is encouraged or not is highly specific to a culture. For example, in European Catholic and Protestant traditions, the custom is that people should grieve quietly and stoically. Still, African, Islamic and Caribbean cultures encourage showing grief openly: for example, by crying loudly.

Moreover, the triggers of different emotions also vary across cultures. For example, in Charles Darwin's classic book, *The Expression of Emotions in Man and Animals*, he writes that things people find disgusting are substantially different in different cultures. Charles Darwin recalls an incident that happened when he was on an expedition to South America as follows:

> *In Tierra del Fuego, there is a native who touched preserved meat he was eating with his fingers while eating at the bivouac and displayed utter disgust at its softness; at the same time, Charles Darwin felt utter disgust at his food being touched by a naked savage although his hands did not appear dirty.*

More presently, psychologists like Feldman Barrett argue that the brain's interpretation regarding certain physiological changes in the body varies across different cultures, situations and individuals. For example, if you win, your emotions create a particular bodily sensation associated with excitement.

Your ability to experience a certain emotion will also depend on your culture. Just like your great-grandmother could not realize a computational device such as a MacBook Pro left behind by a time traveler, you would not also be able to experience jealousy if humans did not have the habit of entering into relationships in which we feel entitled to other people's love, time, and attention.

However, according to a study conducted by emotion researchers, emotional feeling is not subject to similar cultural influence. On the contrary, different emotional feelings are the same when people across different cultures experience them. In determining if different cultures have different ways of feeling emotions, the researchers rounded up participants from 105 countries to read out loud emotions word by word and later colour the area of their body. The colours were based on the feeling when they experienced the emotion in question.

The study aimed to determine how the participants could remember what an emotion feels like. The participants were presented with 13 emotions, including neutral and nonneutral emotional states. Six of the 13 were Ekman's basic emotions (fear, anger, disgust, happiness, sadness, and surprise). At the same time, seven were the non-basic emotions like depression, anxiety, love, shame, contempt, pride and jealousy. When they finished collecting their data, the researchers came up with the markings of activation and those of the activation in a single map for every participant. They then selected 15 countries with at least 45 participants to determine whether their bodily sensations associated with the specific emotion were similar across different cultures.

The study determined that the neutral state and the 13 examined emotions fell into different clusters, called an emotions body signature. This finding was statistically significant across all the tested countries. Although there was cross-cultural variation in how the participants expressed their feeling the emotion was not statistically significant; the researchers found a significant variation between non-westerners and westerners. The study found that westerners had a great activation in different parts of their bodies displaying emotions such as play, love, jealousy, happiness, anxiety, anger, and contempt. At the same time, they were neutral, but non-westerners experienced less deactivation for sadness, depression and shame.

The body signatures for the 13 emotions also varied in gender and age. The intensity of emotional feeling was negatively associated with age, indicating that younger people feel emotions more intensely than older ones. Additionally, compared to men, women had a great activation in their gut during moments of shame, jealousy, anxiety and anger. However, their study found that the overlap of body signatures for emotions was greater than the difference because of age, culture or gender. This means that the extent to which people experience emotions is similar across various cultures. Therefore, the feeling you have when you experience sadness is not majorly different from what people of other cultures experience when they are sad. The study will imply future research on cognitive empathy, also known as "mind-reading." The art of mind reading consists of finding out what other people feel. Therefore, these findings lend support by suggesting that we can reliably use imagination to discover what other people feel like in different emotional states.

Reflections

Identify 3 ways that your culture has influenced your emotions and feelings. Are they positive or negative?

What Happens to Your Emotions When They Move to Other Cultures?

Anyone that has lived in a different culture must have had a cultural shock. Before moving to a different environment, you must have thought that your emotions naturally respond to your environment. Still, when you move to another cultural environment, you realize that you are completely inadequate and hindered by the norms of that culture. After some time, you will start internalizing the emotions of the other culture, and your previous emotions from the previous environment become less prominent. The emotions of the new culture start setting in as default. After a long period of people interacting with other cultures and getting feedback, their emotions are likely to acculturate. Therefore, it is important to know that your emotions are not a natural response but rather cultural, just like other people's emotions. When you interact with people from different cultures, it is important to be aware of each person's emotions by referring to their socialization, norms, and values for proper interaction.

Cultural Differences in Emotional Arousal Level

Cross-cultural differences in emotional arousal levels have consistently been found. Western culture is related to high-arousal emotions, whereas Eastern culture is related to low-arousal emotions. These cultural differences are explained by the distinct characteristics of individualist and collectivist cultures. In Western culture, people try to influence others. For this purpose, high-arousal emotions are ideal and effective. By contrast, in Eastern culture, adjusting and conforming to other people is considered desirable.

The arousal level of *the ideal effect* differs by culture. Ideal affect, or "affective state that people ideally want to feel, is important because people are motivated to behave in certain ways to feel the emotions they want to experience. Therefore, people in certain cultures tend to experience the emotional state considered ideal in their culture.

Furthermore, cultural differences are also found in physiological and behavioural aspects of emotion. Research conducted by Scherer et al. showed that Japanese participants, compared with American and European participants, reported significantly fewer physiological symptoms. Mesquita and Frijda suggested that one possible explanation is that their physiological reactions to emotions differ. In addition, behaviours corresponding to emotional arousal levels differ by culture. Westerners prefer to participate in more active sports than Easterners to elicit high-arousal emotions.

Moreover, parents lead their children to engage in activities likely to elicit valued cultural emotions. For example, Western mothers are reported to encourage their children to play games that increase emotional arousal levels. Therefore, cultural differences in emotional arousal levels emerge relatively young.

Reflections

1. *Have you ever had an emotionally transformative experience while traveling or interacting with people from another culture?*
2. *Identify 2 aspects of culture shock when interacting with another culture or environment. What feelings did you have to the new experience?*

Insights That We Can Gain from Understanding Others' Emotional Lives

1. Since emotions play a central role in our interaction, understanding cultural similarities and differences is critical to preventing miscommunications that can be harmful.

Although misunderstandings are unintentional, they can lead to negative consequences—as seen in minorities in many cultures. For instance, across various North American settings, Asian Americans are often characterized as too "quiet" and "reserved," These low arousal states are usually misinterpreted as expressions of disengagement instead of expressions of the ideal of calmness. On the other hand, Asian Americans may be seen as "cold," "stoic," and "unfriendly," which leads to stereotypes of Asian Americans being termed as "perpetual foreigners" (Cheryan & Monin, 2005). This misunderstanding may be why Asian Americans are often overlooked in top leadership positions (Hyun, 2005).

2. Additionally, recognizing cultural similarities and differences in emotion may provide insights into other psychological health and well-being paths.

For example, some studies suggest that calm states are easier to elicit than excited states. This suggests you can increase happiness in cultures that value excitement by increasing the value placed on calm states (Hogan, & Fung, 2013).

3. According to Philosopher Owen Flanagan, learning about different cultures' philosophies gives you options.

This philosopher holds that you cannot do emotions on yourself, but you do emotions together with others; therefore, emotions are a way of being a person in the social world. However, knowing alternative ways of having emotions through interaction gives you perspectives on dealing with your own emotions.

4. You get a different understanding of your emotions.

For example, an emotion like shame is not so unbearable that we should turn it into anger. This emotion is only unbearable if you have ambitions of being independent and feeling good about yourself, which is a western cultural norm. However, when you interact with Islamic culture, as seen in previous pages, you realize that shame can be bearable. When you experience shame, you can say, "How important is it that I feel good about myself?" If you distance yourself from the cultural goal of feeling self-esteem or independence, you can live with your shame. Having a mindful approach to treating people with deep shame or depression comes from changing your values about what kind of person to be. So, understanding how your emotions are cultured gives you options you don't have otherwise.

Final Take Away

Culture has a profound effect on our emotions. What we feel and how we express those feelings are often determined by the cultural values of the society in which we were raised. However, this is not to say that our emotions are static- on the contrary, they can change dramatically when exposed to new cultures. This diversity of emotion makes cultural interactions valuable- through exposure to different ways of feeling and reacting. We can learn more about ourselves and grow as emotional beings through these experiences.

CHAPTER 6:

EMOTIONS AND OUR MENTAL HEALTH

Our emotional, psychological, and social well-being contributes to our mental health. It has an impact on how we think, feel, and act. In this chapter we shall discuss the relationship between mental health and our emotions, actions and behaviour.

Clarifying Mental Health

Mental health entails cognitive thinking and the ability to focus one's attention, which includes processing information, storing it in memory, and comprehending new information. Processing and reasoning are two important aspects of our personality that affect our mental health. To avoid losing control of our emotions and becoming unstable, we need a strong sense of reasoning. To avoid anxiety or stress, we must carefully consider how we respond to various scenarios. When we lack a balance between processing and reasoning, our health suffers, and we may experience disorientation and difficulty functioning efficiently.

Our emotional, psychological, and social well-being has an impact on how we think, feel, and act. It also influences how we deal with stress, engage with others, and make decisions.

On the other hand, emotions are a key part of our daily lives and emotions may be confusing, and difficult to express constructively for many people, especially when our mental health is compromised.

Reducing the Risk Factors of Mental Health Conditions

Everyone, regardless of age, gender, income, or ethnicity, is at risk of developing a mental health disorder. A person's mental health can be influenced by social and financial circumstances, negative childhood experiences, biological factors, and underlying medical conditions. Many people who have a mental health disorder have multiple conditions at the same time. It is critical to recognize that good mental health depends on a delicate balance of factors and that several factors may contribute to developing these disorders. The following elements can all contribute to mental health problems!

1. Childhood adversity

Child abuse, parental loss, parental separation, and parental illness all harm a growing child's mental and physical health. There are also links between childhood abuse, other traumatic events, and various psychotic disorders. These experiences also put people at risk for post-traumatic stress disorder (PTSD).

2. Constant social and economic pressure

Being poor or belonging to a marginalized ethnic group can increase the risk of mental health disorders, which is true for impoverished people.

3. Biological factors

A person's genetic family history can increase the likelihood of mental health conditions because specific genes and gene variants put them at risk. However, it is important to emphasize that having a gene associated with a mental health disorder does not guarantee the development of the condition. Similarly, people without related genes or a family history of mental illness can still have mental health problems. Chronic stress and mental health conditions like depression and anxiety can arise from underlying physical health issues like cancer, diabetes, and chronic pain.

Good Mental Health Is Instrumental to Our Emotions and How We Act!

1. Good mental health is crucial to accepting and valuing your feelings.

There is frequently a strong relationship between events in your life and your feelings; for example, feeling sad in response to loss or happy in response to something desirable. Feelings can sometimes be linked to past events or even future expectations. For example, grief over a recent loss of a loved one may trigger feelings of sadness, anxiety, and trauma over previous losses. Rather than ignoring or expressing your emotions impulsively, it is important to think about them to learn and improve your reactions.

2. Identifying your feelings becomes easier.

Learning to recognize the link between your feelings and stressors in your life can take time, but it is essential to learn how to deal with emotions healthily.

- Determine the causes of bodily responses and other behavioural patterns. For example, feeling jittery before starting each exam.
- Recognize a bodily reaction to an emotion if you have good mental health. Fear, for example, may cause a knot in your stomach or tightness in your throat, while embarrassment may cause you to blush.

Your mental health has a direct impact on your behaviour. If you don't know how you feel but notice that you're giving off a particular vibe to others, you might be able to deduce what you're feeling from your actions. For example, if you have a frustrated facial expression or tone of voice while speaking with a specific friend, you may be frustrated or angry with that person without realizing it. Making the connection between life events and your emotions is extremely beneficial.

3. Good mental health contributes to better perceptions and interpretations.

While it is natural to believe that you are only reacting to events in your life, you also make interpretations or judgments based on your perceptions of the event or person. When you think about it, each event can elicit a wide range of emotional reactions; your interpretation of such an event helps to connect a specific emotional response to that event.

Your interpretations may appear so fast that you are unaware they are taking place. When your emotional reaction is out of proportion to the event, it is most likely due to your rapid, undetected interpretation of the event rather than the event itself. Further investigation may assist you in gaining perspective on your emotional reactions. Here are some examples of common, recurring self-defeating interpretations caused by poor mental health:

- Dichotomous thinking

You interpret events as extremes. In other words, events are either fantastic or terrible, with no regard for the grey areas in between.

- Excess Personalization

Someone here concludes that another's behaviour or mood is due to them. As a result, when a friend is upset, the person assumes it is their fault.

- Overgeneralization.

This is when a person gives something more weight than it deserves. For example, they may believe they are a bad student because they perform poorly on one test.

- Filtering

It is when we exaggerate negative events while discounting positive ones. For example, a student may only pay attention to one negative comment after a class presentation rather than many positive ones.

- Reasoning based on emotions

It entails confusing your emotions with reality. For example, if you are lonely, you may conclude that you are unworthy of relationships or friends. Recognizing these self-defeating tendencies is difficult, but they do not define you as a person. They can assist us in learning how to express ourselves more accurately and productively.

Reflections

1. *Do you agree that mental health affects our thinking, feelings and perception?*
2. *If you agree that mental health is a key component of emotions, identify 2 incidences where your mental thoughts clouded your perceptions and emotions.*
3. *You stand a better chance of expressing your feelings clearly when you have good mental health.*

Cultural backgrounds, family values, and a variety of other factors can all have an impact on how we express our emotions. We typically learn to express our emotions in two ways: directly expressing them to another person (e.g., through personal confrontation) or hiding the feelings and keeping them to ourselves. Learning to express our emotions in ways consistent with our cultural values while still attending to our needs and feelings can benefit us and our relationships with others.

Consider the case of a close friend who is planning to relocate. This change may make you sad, disappointed, or even irritated. There are numerous ways to respond:

- You might be so upset that you want to avoid your friend until they leave.
- You can keep busy or anxiously pursue new friendships to avoid feeling lonely or sad.

You do have different options for more productively expressing your emotions:

- You could go out of your way to see them before they leave.
- You could tell them you will miss them.

Common Issues Surrounding Mental Health

Mental health deals with behaviours that relate to the mind or brain. Related problems that develop are typically the result of a chemical imbalance in the brain. These issues may include the following:

- Anxiety
- Bipolar disorder
- Depression
- Disordered eating
- PTSD

Early Warning Signs of Poor Mental Health.

Some people may experience mental health issues at some point in their lives, which affect their mood, thinking, and behaviour. According to research, one in every five adults in the United States has a mental illness yearly. There are numerous mental illnesses, each with its symptoms, such as depression, bipolar disorder, and schizophrenia. The following are common signs of mental illness:

- Drug or alcohol abuse
- Experiencing unexplained aches and pains
- Feeling unusually confused, forgetful, agitated, worried, or scared
- Fighting or yelling at family and friends
- Hallucinations
- Having little to no energy
- Having severe mood swings that cause issues in relationships
- Helpless or hopeless feelings
- Inability to perform daily tasks due to insufficient or excessive sleep
- removing oneself from people and routine activities
- Suicidal or harmful ideas

Benefits of Positive Mental Health

- It helps people to achieve their full potential
- People are able to deal with life's stresses
- People tend to work efficiently
- It contributes significantly to the health of communities

Ways of maintaining positive mental health

- Developing coping abilities
- Getting some exercise and helping others
- Getting sufficient sleep
- Keeping a positive attitude

- Making connections with others
- Seeking professional assistance if necessary

Emotional Health

Emotional health is a positive psychological functioning state that includes expressing one's emotions age-appropriately. It is an essential component of overall health. Emotionally healthy people have control over their thoughts, feelings, and behaviours. They are capable of dealing with life's difficulties. They can keep problems in context and recover from setbacks. They are confident in themselves and have positive relationships.

Being emotionally healthy does not imply that you are always happy. It indicates that you are aware of your emotions. You can deal with them regardless of whether they are positive or negative. Emotionally healthy people still experience stress, anger, and sadness. They do, however, know how to deal with their negative emotions. They can recognize when a problem is too big for them to handle. They also know when to seek medical attention.

There are numerous methods for improving or maintaining emotional health. These are some examples:

- Be conscious of your emotions and reactions. Take note of what makes you sad, frustrated, or angry. Make an effort to address or change those issues.
- Consider your options before acting. Allow yourself time to think and be calm before saying or doing something you may regret.

- Control your stress. Learn how to relax to cope with stress. Deep breathing, meditation, and exercise are some examples.
- Discover your life's purpose and meaning. Determine what is most important to you in life and focus on that. It could be your job, family, volunteering, caring for others, or something else. Spend your time doing things that are meaningful to you.
- Express your emotions appropriately. Inform those close to you when something bothers you. Keeping sadness or anger inside increases stress. It can cause issues in your relationships and at work or school.
- Maintain a positive attitude. Concentrate on positive aspects of life. Forgive yourself and others for making mistakes. Spend time with people who are healthy and positive.
- Maintain your physical health. Exercise regularly, eat nutritious foods, and get enough sleep. Don't experiment with drugs or alcohol. Prevent your physical health from interfering with your emotional health.
- Make contact with those around you. Go to lunch dates, introduce yourself to strangers, and join groups or clubs. We require positive interactions with others.
- Strive for equilibrium. Strive for a healthy balance of work and play, as well as activity and rest. Make time for activities that you enjoy. Concentrate on the good things in your life.

Final Take Away

While mental and emotional health is distinct, they are necessary and work together. Stress, fear, anxiety, anger, depression, and worry can all be reduced by effectively managing our mental and emotional health. Humans make many decisions based on feelings because we are constantly bombarded with hundreds of thoughts and emotions. Many of these are generated by cognitive reasoning and processing the current situation. These two distinct but complementary areas of health work together. They ensure our overall health and the ability to communicate and interact effectively with others.

CHAPTER 7:

IDENTIFYING AND DIFFERENTIATING BETWEEN EMOTIONAL NEEDS AND EMOTIONS AND NEEDS

In this chapter, you will understand the difference between our emotions and our emotional needs. This clarity can help us better understand why we feel the way we do, and it can help us take steps toward meeting our emotional needs.

What Are Emotional needs

Everyone has emotional needs. They are an important part of the everyday human experience. As humans, we seek "emotional nourishment" in the same way that we seek food and water. The complexities of meeting these needs may change, especially as we age, but their roots remain constant. So, what are our emotional needs, and how do we meet them? Before we answer these questions, let's first define what emotional needs are in the first place.

Barker in his 2017 publication, describes an emotional need as a condition or state that must be met by yourself or others for you to be peaceful and happy.. When our emotional needs are met and appropriately addressed, we remain in balance. They are necessary for living a healthy lifestyle. We may become frustrated, hurt, or dissatisfied if they are not addressed. Though we all have them, each of us has our own set of emotional needs. Your age, sense of identity, genetic predisposition, culture, upbringing, etc., can contribute to our differences.

Most of us use Maslow's Hierarchy of Needs, a psychology theory developed by Abraham Maslow in 1943, to describe the most fundamental human emotional needs. His hierarchy demonstrates the progression. The primary needs are at the bottom of the pyramid, and the most complex needs are at the top; Food and water are at the bottom, while self-actualization is at the top. Based on this understanding, research has expanded to identify nine specific emotional needs shared by people of all cultures.

The nine basic emotional needs are listed below, along with actions that you can leverage to help ensure they are met!

1. Sense of Achievement

Humans require something to strive for. We can recognize, analyze, problem-solve, imagine, create, and strive. We begin to criticize ourselves when we believe we are not achieving a goal. As a result, we may lose motivation and become lazy, believing that we cannot achieve our goals.

Action Plan: List all your notable accomplishments, both big and small. Examine your diplomas, promotions, awards, and scholarships. Consider your healthy gains, such as quitting smoking, losing weight, or fixing your teeth. Make a list of any heartbreaks or rough patches you've endured. Then go back over what you've written and list the skills you had or learned that helped you achieve these goals. Increase your awareness of your accomplishments to inspire you to find new things to accomplish.

2. Sense of Self

Being a part of a community or group is important, but so is understanding your value within the group dynamic. We need to understand that we play an important and distinct role within the structure. People frequently confuse having a strong sense of self with being a leader or an extrovert. It really means understanding your position within a social group and understanding how important it is to the group.

Action Plan: Create more opportunities to distinguish yourself from your peers. It could be taking on a new role at work, researching trivia questions for an upcoming game night with friends, or even volunteering to organize the next play-date schedule.

3. Community Connection

Our brains are social organs connecting us to something bigger than ourselves. That fundamental need enables you to give way to something other than your desires, deepening your experience of fulfilled intention.

Action Plan: Volunteer or give back to your community through philanthropy. If volunteering is not an option, you can help someone in your field by mentoring them. You could be qualified to teach or coach if you possess specialized skill sets.

4. Intimacy

Humans are social beings. Loneliness, isolation, and dissociation are exacerbated by disconnection. Having an emotionally attuned connection with others lets us know that we are not alone but also desired and sought after. Emotional intimacy is a deep realization that we are accepted as we are.

Action Plan: If you're feeling lonely in your relationships, consider what needs to be addressed to foster more emotional intimacy. Increase sharing of your hopes, dreams, and desires, for example. If you discover that you cannot be vulnerable, investigate the source of the problem.

5. Attention

Feeling valued requires giving and receiving quality contact with others and oneself. This contact can take the form of affection or validation, or it can be as simple as acknowledging the existence of a purpose.

Action Plan: Check in with those important to you, including yourself, to learn what is required to foster healthy attention. Then, make an effort to cultivate meaningful interactions with friends, family, and partner/s. It's also important to make time for yourself and incorporate more self-care activities.

6. Volition

Humans require the feeling that we can choose how we live. We strive to be in charge of our own lives and live independently.

Action Plan: Identify the situations and people that make you feel powerless. Take the time to learn assertive communication to establish clear boundaries with these people and those situations.

7. Privacy

Humans require time and space to live a balanced lifestyle and learn from our experiences. Some people, particularly introverts, empaths, and people sensitive to overstimulation, require more decompression than others.

Action Plan: Begin your day by reflecting on and planning for the tasks ahead. Rehearse any situations you know that may lead to reactivity during this morning's reflection. You can also use mediation to achieve your goals and intentions for yourself and your loved ones. Finally, journaling is a great way to express yourself and learn from your mistakes.

8. Security

People require a safe environment in which to live their lives. It enables us to reach our full potential. These safe havens can be physical, emotional, or spiritual.

Action Plan: Make a list of what makes you feel insecure or threatened in your environment. Once you've identified them, list actionable steps to eliminate or modify those factors. Installing a burglary system, for example, can help reduce the fear of being robbed.

9. Meaning

Humans need to have coherent beliefs about life and what it's all for. We have to have a core set of values, at least one guiding us to a sense of purposeful belonging. Basically, we need to feel like we have an answer to the question of "why we're here."

Action Plan: If you're feeling apathetic about life or questioning your overall existence, incorporating mindfulness, present-moment experiences, and body awareness is critical to reconnecting with meaning. It can be as simple as noticing how your breath fills your lungs, nourishes your body, and reminds you that you are whole. You can also find meaning by supporting a cause, discovering political ideologies that speak to you, or learning what it means to take on new familial roles, such as parenthood.

Reflections

1. *Which 2 of these emotional needs do you meet often?*
2. *Which 2 of these emotional needs do you need to work on? Define your action plan.*

Emotional nourishment is required for humans to function fully. It enables us to coexist peacefully within a family, a group, and a community. When circumstances in our lives interfere with our ability to meet these needs, we experience significant distress. As a result, it's critical to identify which emotional needs aren't being met and to take action to address them. It can help to understand why your needs have taken such a back seat in your life as you begin to connect more with them. When we understand why we struggle with something, we are better positioned to "fix" it.

People who instinctively understand their needs do so because they have experienced them. If you're having trouble identifying your needs right now, it is likely certain needs were not met by your family and other loved ones adequately as you grew up.

Assume you grew up with a parent who was distant or aloof. It means you and others in your family rarely expressed emotions openly, and you learned that it was better to keep them bottled up. It may be why you're having difficulty identifying and expressing your needs right now.

Emotions and Needs

Gläser-Zikuda defines emotions as a set of interconnected processes that include subjective feelings, cognitive appraisals, physiological factors, expressive behaviour and characteristics, and motivational tendencies, in her 2012 journal article. They are fundamental psychological systems that govern an individual's response to personal and environmental demands. Emotions help you meet your needs because they help you survive, allowing you to distinguish between a good and a bad situation. They also encourage you to effectively relate to and communicate with others.

One of the primary functions of emotions is to physiologically prepare you for survival. For instance, if you see an approaching snake, your body will react even before you consider whether it is poisonous or not. In this case, your heart rate will increase to send more blood to your muscles, allowing you to escape the potential danger. This way, if you need to get out of a situation quickly, you'll act rather than think. Others can tell how you perceive and interpret internal and external stimuli based on your emotions.

Emotions can assist you in determining whether or not you like a particular situation. As a result, depending on how you feel, you'll want to repeat or avoid the experience. They function as an internal compass, assisting you in orienting yourself and determining what is truly important.

Every emotion is important!

Every emotion serves a purpose, and they are all valid and necessary. They're your traveling companions; they'll accompany you wherever you go and tell you what you need to know. Would you know what makes you happy if it weren't for joy? Would you defend yourself if you didn't feel angry? Women and people in general, struggle with the complicated concept of emotions and needs. Identifying emotions, understanding emotions, and expressing emotions are all daily struggles.

Understanding emotion can assist us in overcoming these challenges because it leads to the following:

1) Enhanced empathy communication abilities

Listening and communicating leads to reduce conflicts, misunderstandings, and miscommunication.

2) Greater empathy.

Connection with other people's feelings and a desire to know and understand them better.

3) Greater self-awareness

Being clear about our needs and directing our behaviour accordingly.

Real-life examples to help you understand the link between your emotions, needs, and, consequently, your actions

1. You have communication and closeness needs with your friends. You call them, but they do not answer the phone, and you feel depressed.
2. You value education, so you keep a routine to complete your college assignments on time. However, the internet goes down just as you're about to submit an assignment, and now you're panicking and worried that you'll miss the deadline.
3. You're having difficulty with a work project and you require assistance and consideration. You seek assistance from a coworker. They offer you advice and assistance, and you feel grateful.

From the examples above, it is clear that at any given time, we have needs that may cause us to experience certain emotions, and to meet these needs, we may resort to actions or inactions. Those actions may turn out to be healthy or unhealthy in the long run, but emotions are neither good nor bad in and of themselves. The better we understand the cyclical relationship between needs, emotions, and actions, the more we can connect with ourselves and others.

The Basic Concept of Needs

As per Cherry's 2022 publication on behavioural psychology, Maslow correctly explained in his hierarchy of needs pyramid that everyone has different needs and that you are motivated by the need to fulfill them. Humans have two kinds of basic needs: physical and spiritual. Most of us know the basic survival needs of food, clothing, shelter, and protection. Sexual expression, rest, sleep, exercise, water, air, and the touch of other living beings are examples of other physical needs.

Spiritual needs are more complex and, unlike physical needs, can be difficult to assess whether they are being met. It is critical for personal growth and freedom to be able to connect feelings to spiritual needs. Humans have fundamental spiritual requirements for beauty, harmony, inspiration, order, and peace.

Some spiritual needs overlap with physical requirements; belonging, order, communication, exploration and orientation, are examples of these needs. The interaction of these needs results in behavioural tendencies. For example, your spiritual need to belong to your place and time, family, and community manifests itself in your values, goals, and dreams.

Furthermore, your need to belong influences your choices regarding your marriage partner, housing, clothing, and so on, and may include your needs for understanding, trust, respect, love, honesty, emotional safety, appreciation, and so on. Examining our links between needs and behaviour can help clarify the relationship between feelings and needs.

When you connect your needs to your feelings, behaviours, and actions, it will be much easier to accept responsibility for your actions and intentions. You will also realize that you are not responsible for the feelings of others, and your decisions may no longer be based on avoiding someone's disappointment. Emotional liberation is the fruit of emotional responsibility, which many people seek to emotionally empower themselves.

Effective Techniques to Regulate Your Emotions

As much as the overall idea is to let your emotions guide you, you must ensure that they do so correctly. Never let your emotions get the best of you, and pay attention to your thoughts too. Do not become so overwhelmed by emotions that your mind wanders off course. This is why learning to manage your emotions is so important. Here are some practical techniques you can leverage to help you out.

1. Identify

Being aware of your emotions will undoubtedly help you manage them. Knowing how to tell if you're sad or angry, for example, and distinguishing between the concrete situation or the thought that caused the emotion will allow you to act appropriately. Furthermore, being aware of your emotions can help you identify them in others, making you more empathetic.

2. Tolerate

Even though some emotions, such as sadness and anger, are considered negative, it is critical to learn to tolerate them rather than avoid them. Emotions come and go; it's all part of the process. If you're depressed right now, it doesn't mean you'll be depressed forever or that you're a depressed person. Avoid blocking or suppressing your emotions; pay attention to them, feel them, and learn to cope.

3. Self-regulate

We can all regulate ourselves. Don't just let the feeling pass you by; do something about it! Try your hardest to keep negative thoughts at bay and focus on the bright side of things. Distract yourself or do something enjoyable to reduce the intensity of your emotions. Improve yourself by learning to control your impulses. You'll be taking care of yourself while also improving your overall health.

4. Express yourself and communicate

You should rely on your resources and express your emotions to those around you too. It is important to express emotions. Trust others and communicate your feelings and needs to them.

Reflections

1. *Think about the last time you felt emotionally overwhelmed. How did you manage your emotions?*
2. *Consider the 4 steps detailed above on how to regulate your emotions. How can you use them the next time?*

Understanding Emotional Intelligence and Differentiation Concepts

This will help to easily differentiate between emotional needs and "emotions and needs."

Emotional Intelligence (EI)

Draghici (2022) states that emotional intelligence (EI) is the ability of a person to understand manage and recognize their emotions and those of others. It is a valuable tool because it facilitates our capacity for communication, stress management, reasoning, empathy, resilience, motivation, and navigating various conflicts and social situations.

Emotional intelligence is also a key part of successful relationships and overall well-being. It is the ability to understand and recognize our own feelings, as well as those of others around us. With emotional intelligence, we are better equipped to process emotions in ourselves, respond appropriately to other people's feelings, and handle conflicts and stresses of daily life. This allows us to develop better communication skills and social understanding and foster healthy relationships with those around us. Further, emotional intelligence can help strengthen our mental health by enabling us to stay in tune with ourselves and identify destructive thought patterns before they become overwhelming. This makes it essential for personal development and happiness – both inside and outside of the workplace. Ultimately, having emotional intelligence can be a major factor in making our home lives more harmonious and making us more productive at work.

Components of Emotional Intelligence

1. Self-awareness is the ability to recognize and comprehend one's emotions and their impact on others. You know your skills and flaws and are self-assured when connecting to your feelings. Understanding how

emotion affects your beliefs and behaviours requires having a moment-to-moment connection with your shifting emotional experience.
2. Self-management is regulating impulsive sentiments and behaviours, healthily managing your emotions, taking the initiative, following through on commitments, and adapting to changing circumstances.
3. Self-regulation refers to managing negative or disruptive emotions and adapting to changing circumstances.
4. Motivation is the ability to motivate oneself as well as others.
5. Empathy is the ability to recognize and comprehend how others feel. You can comprehend other people's feelings, wants, and problems, pick up on emotional clues, feel at ease socially, and identify power dynamics in a group or organization.
6. Relationship management - You understand how to build and maintain positive relationships, communicate effectively, inspire and influence people, collaborate effectively, and handle conflict.
7. Social awareness is the skill that allows you to manage other people's emotions through emotional understanding.

If you have a high EI, you have enough self-awareness to recognize negative feelings and respond appropriately to prevent them from escalating. It is a necessary skill for overall well-being. With low EI, you will experience misunderstood and uncontrollable emotions, easily exacerbating vulnerability to other mental health issues such as depression, stress, and anxiety.

Emotional Differentiation

Emotion differentiation is the propensity to differentiate among one's own emotions and to label one's emotions in a discrete, context-sensitive manner. According to Vedernikova et al. (2021), a "low differentiator" may report feeling both sad and anxious in all situations, whereas a "high differentiator" may report feeling different emotions in different situations, such as sad and guilty in response to one event and anxiety, overwhelmed, and disappointment in response to another. Emotional differentiation allows for more effective emotion regulation. Higher levels of emotion differentiation, for example, protected individuals from destructive behaviour such as aggression, poor eating habits, and excessive alcohol consumption.

Positive emotion differentiation is linked to more thought, resulting in more behavioural options before acting, less automatic responding, more effective coping styles, higher engagement in the coping process, and less mental self-distraction during stressful times. Higher differentiation also appeared to be beneficial in interpersonal relationships, as it was associated with greater empathic accuracy and better recognition of others' emotional expressions.

Final Take Away

Understanding our emotional needs and our "emotions and needs" allows us to be happy and can alleviate feelings of helplessness. We can take a fresh look at the imbalances in our relationships, jobs, and environment. Instead of assuming something is "wrong" with us, we can ask, "What emotional needs are not being met?" When you meet these needs in balance, you realize you have more power in your own life and that the journey to meeting these needs and helping others meet theirs in your relationships, occupations, and communities can be very fulfilling in and of itself.

PART 2:
WHAT IS EMOTIONAL EMPOWERMENT

CHAPTER 1:

WHAT EMOTIONAL EMPOWERMENT IS NOT

In this chapter you will learn what the lack of emotional intelligence is. It will assist you in identifying circumstances in yourself or in others that suggest a low emotional quotient. You'll use that awareness to make an effort to improve your emotional reactions and progressively gain emotional empowerment.

What is Low EQ?

Low emotional intelligence is the inability to effectively recognize emotions (in oneself and others) and utilize that information to influence one's thoughts and actions which present themselves in many ways. The emotional reactions that result from interactions with these individuals can be draining and frustrating and may cause us to repel or dread any associations.

People with low EQ typically tend to come across as abrasive and insensitive and hence have very few close friends; since close friendships require mutual emotional support and sharing, which low-EQ persons generally lack. Individuals with low EQ lack empathy, struggle to manage their emotions and are unable to comprehend other people's feelings.

How To Know When You Have Low EQ

Have you felt like you can't seem to connect with people the way others do? or do you find yourself constantly offended by comments that don't seem harmful to others? If so, you may be dealing with low EQ. Emotional intelligence is essential in life, work, and relationships, so it's important to identify when you or someone is not performing at their best. Here are some key factors that tell if one needs to work on their emotional intelligence.

1. They Must Always Be 'Right' and Are Highly Opinionated

Individuals with low emotional quotients constantly get into fights with others, even strangers, due to their argumentative nature. They usually argue a point to death and refuse to accept other people's perspectives; for them, it is either their way or the highway! Even when presented with proof of their error, they will always argue that those facts are invalid. They must win at all costs, especially if others are critical of how the individual does not comprehend how others feel. They tend to dwell on their errors and have difficulty learning from them and moving on.

2. They Lack Empathy and Behave Insensitively.

People with poor emotional quotient cannot distinguish between suitable and inappropriate times to make certain statements, making situations awkward. They cannot perceive and correctly respond to the present emotional tone and mood because they have difficulties understanding the feelings of others, even when style brings up their unacceptable behaviour.

For example, they may say something offensive or make a joke immediately following a devastating occurrence and become defensive, acting as though you're unduly sensitive if you react to their out-of-line response.

Reflections

1. Do you tend to be the one who must win an argument?
2. Have you ever been in a situation where someone or you made an inappropriate or lousy joke that offended those around you?

3. They Have Narcissistic Tendencies: Self-Centeredness

Emotionally ignorant personalities seek to be the center of attention at all times; therefore, they tend to dominate every discourse. Even if they appear to be asking questions and listening closely, they always find a way to bring everything back to them.

They're easy to detect since they're doing most of the talking. They usually have to establish that whatever you're going through, they've been through it before, for better or worse.

Their experiences appear superior to everyone else's and seem to have done that. Their achievements are more exceptional than yours, and their downfalls are more devastating and dramatic than yours.

Cherry K simplifies this in an example:

> *Whatever you say, they've been there and done that. Have you been in a vehicle accident? They did, too, and their dog perished as a result. Are you planning to climb Mount Kilimanjaro? Four years ago, they scaled Mount Everest. If you wish, they can email you a list of tips and suggestions for success!*

4. They Blame Others For Their Problems and Lack Accountability

People with low emotional intelligence frequently cause difficulties because they have difficulty comprehending the situations of others and always want to be correct. They refuse to accept responsibility for the consequences of their conduct and therefore never hold themselves accountable for their actions.

When something goes wrong, their immediate instinct is to blame someone or something else. A person with low EQ may claim that they had no option but to do what they did. Others do not comprehend their circumstances and protect themselves by informing everyone that they are misunderstood.

For example, *suppose you had several assignments from a class and you must complete it as a group within a fair amount of time. Each of you got a part to work on, but you delegated them to others to help you complete. They got busy and could not commit to your work and neglected their duties and made sure to communicate the fact to you early enough. But because you relaxed thinking they would come through, you procrastinate till a few days before the deadline and panic. In your defence, you claim that it is not your responsibility since other people committed to helping you out on your parts, so they are to blame. They initially said they would help; furthermore, they had enough time.*

Reflection

1. How do you feel when someone takes over your conversation and makes their experiences seem better or worse than yours?
2. Ever encountered or blamed others for situations for which you should take responsibility?

5. Unpredictable Emotional Outbursts and Poor Self-Regulation

One component of emotional intelligence is the capacity to manage emotions. People with low emotional intelligence have difficulty controlling, understanding, and expressing their feelings. They may respond irrationally, not comprehending what they are genuinely experiencing or why they are so unhappy.

People with poor EQ may also have frequent, sudden emotional outbursts that appear exaggerated and uncontrollable. They are readily aroused by minor problems, irritating them and forcing them to lash out for hours.

Reflections

1. Does this describe someone you know?
2. Chances are, the person has poor emotional intelligence.

3. *Do you know someone who never seems to be able to keep their emotions under control?*
4. *Maybe they're always doing or saying the wrong thing at the incorrect moment?*
5. *Or perhaps they are constantly judging people yet have difficulty receiving criticism?*

How to Self- Analyze your Emotions

To achieve or determine emotional maturity, Cindy Lamothe, in a Healthline article, opines that you can ask yourself some of the following fundamental questions:

1. **How did you handle a recent tense situation?**

Consider your behaviours and facial expressions when confronted with a difficult circumstance or under pressure to perform. Do you lash out at others, or do you engage in stress-relieving activities like going to the gym, spring cleaning, or gardening?

It is critical to step away from whatever is giving you stress; being irritated with others while failing to recognize your own needs is an indication that you may need to work on your maturity.

2. **How have you handled unexpected change?**

Consider your reaction when individuals around you advance or beautiful things happen to them. Did you wish them well and inquire how you might assist them in their celebration, or did you retreat and feel irritated with them for divulging information? People with emotional maturity may show their happiness to others even in adversity.

3. **Are you frequently irritated by everyone and everything?**

When you're younger, the world is full of petty annoyances, and you're oblivious to your rights. Consider how frequently you criticize individuals or different events in a day. Do you express appreciation or review everything that has gone wrong? Can you see how others' situations may be worse?

4. **Do you usually blame yourself or others when things go wrong?**

Being consumed with self-blame or finding fault with everyone around you is an indication that you need to work on your maturity. Learning to perceive a situation with self-compassion and subtlety when nothing is black or white might help you avoid getting caught up in the blame game.

Improving Emotional Intelligence

Relationships at work and at home need a lot of time and effort to be successful, especially if they involve people with different backgrounds or lifestyles. One great way to improve your relationships is by developing your emotional intelligence. Those who have mastered emotional intelligence can often improve their relationships with family members, friends, and colleagues. Do not be disheartened if you notice that yours is down, Kendra Cherry suggests a variety of ways to improve it:

1. **Learn to Listen**

The first step in understanding what other people are feeling is to pay attention. Take the time to hear what others are saying to you, both orally and nonverbally, to pick up where they struggle with coping challenges. Body language may convey a lot of information. Consider the various things that may be contributing to someone's emotion when you notice them feeling a specific way to assist them in being more self-aware. Teach children to reflect on and digest their feelings and experiences.

2. Be the Bigger Person

Respect and appreciate each person's distinct personality types and how difficult it is for them to change. It will benefit you and the other person to devise a strategy for achieving self-awareness; hence recognize the part you play and accept the circumstances.

3. Empathize

Picking up on emotions is essential, but you must also be able to put them into context by putting yourself in other people's shoes to grasp their point of view genuinely.

She suggests an experimental approach to empathizing with others that involves considering how you would react if you were in their shoes. Such exercises can assist in developing an emotional knowledge of a given circumstance and gaining more extraordinary emotional abilities in the long run.

4. Ask questions and listen

This will help to learn about one another - everyone has their own unique experience.

5. Start journaling

Write out your feelings, directly connecting physical sensations to events or experiences.

6. **Practice self-management techniques**

These include deep breathing when feeling overwhelmed. You can also walk away when you get angry to avoid saying hurtful things to your children and others.

Reflections

Emotional intelligence includes the capacity to reason with emotions. Consider the role that other people's emotions play when considering how they respond.

1. *What is causing this person to feel this way?*
2. *Is there anything else that might be causing these feelings?*
3. *How are your feelings different from theirs?*

By exploring these areas of improvement, individuals can become more aware of how their emotions affect their own behaviour and the behaviour of those around them - leading to better relationships all around!

How to Embrace Emotions and Get to the Next Level

Accepting that we are experiencing unpleasant feelings, identifying why we are experiencing them, and allowing ourselves to hear the lessons they are teaching us are essential to letting them go and moving on.

1. Learn how to effectively articulate your feelings, which you may do by journaling and communicating with others who empower and support you.
2. To effectively embrace emotions, we must embrace our actual sentiments and the repercussions of each and allow

for adjustment if required. Unmanaged rage, for example, might push us to ruin relationships if we allow it.
3. Start attending to your emotional needs by scheduling time for things that make you joyful and healthily manage your stress.
4. Recognize the probability of failure. When we are frightened of failure, we never learn from our errors. This fear impedes the ability to achieve better well-being and resilience as a woman.
5. Make happiness a non-negotiable aim rather than a rigid one. When you focus all of your attention on pursuing happiness, you will recognize when you are truly happy.

Ask yourself every day;

1. *What inspires me?*
2. *Is it because it makes me happy?*
3. *What meaning does it give to my life?*

While it is essential to keep a cheerful attitude in theory, it is also necessary to realize that negative things will come to us from time to time. The idea is not to avoid unpleasant sensations but rather to deal with them healthily. *"It's vital that we as humans build our capacity to cope with our ideas and emotions in a manner that doesn't seem like a battle, in a way that accepts, engages with, and can learn from them,"* Susan David adds.

3 Tips for Dealing with Difficult Emotions in A Healthy Way

Everyone experiences difficult emotions, such as anger, fear, sadness and anxiety. While it's normal to feel this way sometimes, there are steps you can take to deal with those emotions in a healthy way.

1. Talk about these feelings with someone you trust.

Don't bottle your feelings up. By speaking to someone else, you release the energy of your emotions and provide closure.

2. Practice mindful breathing

This helps to bring yourself back into the present moment and create perspective on your feelings.

3. Recognize that these challenging feelings will pass eventually

Situations and emotions change over time — and allow yourself time to process and move through them without judgment. Most importantly, be gentle with yourself during this process: You are allowed to take the time necessary for healing and for finding ways of engaging with difficult emotions in a constructive manner.

All of these things combined should help you emerge from difficult emotional moments feeling more balanced and resilient.

Reflections

From experience, what was a negative reaction to a person or situation that made you angry or sad?
1. *What was the outcome?*
2. *Would you react the same to that situation now?*
3. *What would you do differently now?*

Final Take Away

Emotional intelligence is something that can be developed and improved over time with practice. As women, we have a unique opportunity to use our emotional intelligence to create better relationships in our personal lives and in the workplace.

CHAPTER 2:

EMOTIONAL MATURITY

This chapter will look at some key indicators of emotional maturity in women. We will also look at some practices to help women cultivate an active awareness of emotions and grow in emotional maturity.

What Emotional Maturity Looks Like

Emotionally mature people can manage their emotions regardless of their circumstances. They understand how to respond to adversity while remaining calm. It's a skill set that they can hone over time. When we think of someone who is emotionally mature, we usually see someone aware of their own identity. Even if they don't have all the answers, emotionally mature people exude "peace amid the storm." They are the ones we turn to when facing a difficult situation because they perform well under pressure.

Emotional maturity entails being aware of and controlling one's own emotions, prejudices, biases, and privileges and demonstrating empathy and compassion for the feelings and reactions of those around us. It is not easy to achieve emotional maturity. It can imply confronting aspects of ourselves that we have previously chosen to ignore, admitting past mistakes, and being open about our true thoughts and feelings. It also entails being gentle with yourself and letting go of what you regret.

Notably, emotional maturity is a constant work in progress; therefore, one cannot attain a specific level of self-awareness once and remain static in all future situations. However, one must know what they can bring emotionally when dealing with any circumstances. It's also crucial to understand that not everyone will always be able to respond with emotional maturity in every scenario. When confronted with a challenging scenario, not everyone can maintain their composure at all times

Cindy Lamothe proposes the following strategies for achieving emotional maturity:

1. Accept Responsibility and Own Up to Mistakes

People who have attained emotional maturity are aware of their contributions to the world and will make an effort to adjust their behaviour when the situation demands. An emotionally mature individual can accept responsibility for their faults rather than complaining and blaming others. When things go wrong, they evaluate the circumstances to see what they can improve to avoid similar undesirable occurrences and immediately apologize in an attempt to resolve the problem. Doing so indicates that they have a humble spirit and require self-awareness and self-acceptance.

They do not feel the need always to be right; instead, they admit to not having all the answers, proving an understanding of what they don't know, and that their method of doing things may not be the only or even the best way. An emotionally mature individual will not dispute "simply to be right" or demonstrate superiority to be in charge. They retain an open mind and open ears and eyes to search for circumstances where they may learn something new and recognize when they have something constructive to contribute to a situation that might assist others.

Reflection

1. *Have you been in an emotionally engaging conflict that continued to go wrong no matter how you tried to solve it with the other party?*
2. *What steps did you take to remedy the situation?*
3. *Why do you believe they did not yield the desired results?*
4. *Did you find yourself searching within to see where you were at fault or contributed to the unresolved conflict?*
5. *What steps did you take to change your thoughts or behaviour that worked to remedy the situation?*

2. They Demonstrate Empathy

Individuals who are emotionally mature approach life by doing as much good as possible and helping people around them. They are open-minded and prefer to communicate with people and show genuine empathy for others by being frequently concerned about people and seeking methods to assist them. These individuals avoid being judgmental, often based on preconceived assumptions, which might hamper their capacity to know someone and their truth.

Reflections:

1. *Have you been in a situation that required you to show empathy?*
2. *Would you say you were open-minded and approachable in that situation?*
3. *In a difficult emotional argument, would you immediately become judgmental based on a one-sided view, or would you seek to understand another person's perspective?*
4. *Given a second chance to work out a difficult situation with a family member or friend, what would you do differently?*

3. Be Fearless of Being Vulnerable.

Emotionally mature people are constantly eager to discuss their problems with others to help them feel less lonely. They don't want to be viewed as "perfect" all of the time, but they openly admit that they too often falter. Emotional maturity entails being honest about your feelings and building trust with others, especially if you have no ulterior motives.

Consequently, when confronted with setbacks, situations of distress or disappointment, an emotionally mature person remains resilient, accepts their feelings, determines what can be done, and then decides how to proceed.

Reflections

1. *Are you the person in your circle that people consider the go-to solid person for emotional strength?*
2. *Have you found yourself in a situation of emotional vulnerability?*
3. *Did you discuss the situation or try to hide your emotions to avoid appearing weak?*

4. Recognize and Accept Your Needs

Those who are emotionally mature may confess when they need help or are on the verge of burnout.

For example, you'll recognize when you need a break and know when to request a day off from your supervisor. When you're overwhelmed by pressure to beat deadlines, you know that you can confidently delegate some duties to avoid being overwhelmed.

We all have fundamental emotional requirements. Some of these are universal, while others may be specific to you. As we learnt before, there are five basic emotional requirements as proposed by Jeffrey Young, Schema Therapy in 2003. These are:

1. The need to feel secure
2. The need to have autonomy, competence, and a feeling of identity
3. The ability to articulate our wants and emotions
4. To behave impulsively and to have fun
5. Having realistic limitations aids us in exercising self-control.

To recognize your emotional requirements, make a list under each of these headings as you consider the following questions:

- What would make me feel safe and secure in life?
- What would give me a feeling of purpose, autonomy, and identity?
- How much play and fun do I have in my life right now?

5. **They Set Healthy Boundaries**

Setting healthy limits demonstrates self-love and respect. Knowing when and how to draw a line and not allowing others to cross it indicates that you're emotionally mature. If someone insults or dismisses you, you will not tolerate it, but speak out.

6. **They are Composed**

Emotionally mature individuals become angry, but they do not allow emotion to determine their reaction. They strive to have a clear mind to give room for reason to dictate how to deal with a problem correctly and understand the possibilities of reaching a successful resolution. They know that when emotions take precedence over logic, clarity of mind becomes hazy, limiting their alternatives for responding successfully.

How Women Can Become Emotionally Mature

Emotional intelligence and maturity are complicated notions that change as we get older and exposed to new settings. Understanding the distinction and assessing where we are might offer new possibilities for how we develop, sustain, or salvage relationships. To attain emotional intelligence, women could:

1. **Learn to separate emotions from reactions.**

Emotional maturity results from being aware of and controlling one's emotions. This ability can significantly impact your interactions with others because you can create a gap between your initial emotion and your immediate reaction rather than feeling an emotion and reacting immediately.

2. **Be mindful.**

Mindfulness can help women become more aware of their thoughts and feelings and gain control over their emotions. It can also help you appreciate the little things in life and relieve the pressure of striving for happiness if you're constantly striving for perfection.

Growing in emotional maturity can significantly impact your well-being and relationships with others. Mindfulness practice, learning from past experiences, and opening your mind to learning something new are essential steps toward emotional maturity.

3. **Be willing to learn**

Being open to learning is an integral part of developing emotional maturity. An emotionally mature person recognizes that they do not know everything and that there is always more to learn and gain from those around them. It is acceptable to admit that we do not have all the answers and require guidance from time to time, whether from a therapist, teacher, or friend. By broadening your horizons, you will be able to grow in more ways than one.

4. **Think about previous reactions.**

When we consider our emotional maturity level, we frequently recall times in our lives of which we are not proud. Perhaps previous disagreements, negative opinions we've held about others, or when we let our fears and anxieties get the best of us. While this can be upsetting, it can be beneficial to reflect on these situations and retrospectively practice emotional maturity. Personal reflexivity allows us to become aware of our prejudices and biases and recognize how empathy may have influenced our reactions.

Tonya Lester LCSW identifies three critical points about emotionally mature people to consider in her article, *"Staying Sane Inside Insanity."*

- Emotionally mature people accept complete responsibility for their feelings, reactions, and lives.
- Emotionally mature people can feel empathy for both themselves and others at the same time.
- People who are emotionally mature speak up and tell the truth, even when it is difficult.

Reflection

1. *Do you believe you are on the right path towards emotional maturity?*
2. *What is your maturity level on a scale of 0-10?*
3. *How would you improve your reactions to attain a certain degree of maturity?*
4. *What additional factors will contribute to women's emotional maturity journey?*

Five Benefits of Having High Emotional Maturity as a Woman

Women with high emotional intelligence are at an advantage in many areas; understanding, interpreting, and reacting to emotions can benefit a person in both personal and professional settings. Here are five exceptional benefits of having high emotional intelligence as a woman:

1. **Better Managers of Tough Situations**

Women with strong emotional intelligence can often handle intense situations more effectively than those without them. They are better able to stay calm, think clearly, and make decisions based on sound judgment instead of impulsiveness.

2. **They Build Stronger Relationships**

Women with high emotional intelligence have the social skills to build stronger relationships and use effective communication techniques when faced with difficult conversations.

3. **They are More Self Aware**

This heightened self-awareness helps them achieve higher levels of personal growth especially as they practice mindfulness on a daily basis.

4. **They display leadership qualities**

Women who are emotionally intelligent often navigate conflicts successfully while inspiring others around them.

5. **They are Happier!**

Having mastery over one's emotions can bring immense satisfaction when it comes to experiencing joy more frequently in their life.

Women with strong emotional intelligence certainly stand out from the crowd and reap many benefits because of this ability! Mentally and emotionally sound individuals demonstrate resilience in the face of adversity, making them powerful sources of inspiration for young girls looking for role models who radiate strength even during times of struggle. The capacity for being emotionally brilliant is worth taking time to cultivate!

Final Take Away

It's never too late for any woman to begin practicing her own brand of self-mastery through the art of emotional self-care. With effort comes progress; harnessing higher levels of emotional intelligence can open new doors for any strong-willed woman out there striving for success! Bring your own level of EQ into every room you enter - let your strength shine through!

CHAPTER 3:

WOMEN WHO HAVE SHOWN GREAT EMOTIONAL EMPOWERMENT

Have you ever heard the saying, "There's a new woman in town?" This chapter is about women who have taken charge and shown emotional empowerment. These ladies are bright, passionate and ambitious. They know who they are, practice emotional maturity and are empowered. So, if you're looking for some inspiration, read on!

World Class Emotionally Empowered Women

1. **Hillary Clinton**

Many women have faced infidelity in one way or the other, pushing them to consider if their love (and their partner) is more than trust or stronger than betrayal. Hillary Clinton, a former US secretary of state, First Lady, and Democratic presidential aspirant, is no exception.

In 1992, her husband, the then president of the United States, Bill Clinton, was accused of having an extramarital affair with Monica

Lewinsky. It led to his impeachment and later exoneration. Despite her husband's infidelity, her decision to stay in her marriage elicited mixed reactions. Most of the criticism came from women, primarily because they saw staying in a relationship post-affair as essentially allowing him to do it to you again, whereas leaving is the applauded decision for one's self-respect and physical well-being.

Her decision did not go without consequences, as she was confronted with these realities when she put herself up to run for president. She faced much criticism even though she's not the only woman in America who has ever concluded that an imperfect relationship with a flawed guy is in her best interests. She admitted that she loves someone who has wounded her and that her relationship requires effort for it to operate.

She showed great emotional strength when she agreed to open up about everything in her life by featuring in a four-part documentary that forced her to confront the painful and public issue surrounding her husband's infidelity and her decision to stay.

Regarding her decision, she told Ellen DeGeneres. "People must think carefully about the decisions they make in their own life, and we must be nicer and more supportive to everyone who makes the best judgments they believe they can make."

The stigma surrounding her decision and the subsequent uproar only proved that none of the criticism about why she stayed had anything to do with the difficulties confronting America except to argue that a woman's acceptance of a defective guy into her personal life should have professional consequences.

2. Graca Machel of Mozambique, Africa

Graça Machel is the widow of former President of Mozambique Samora Machel (1975-1986), who later married former President of South Africa Nelson Mandela (1998-2013).

Machel is a global human rights activist, a Minister of Education in Mozambique and the Founder of the Graça Machel Trust (GMT). This woman is among the world's lead advocates for children and women's rights and has also been a social justice and political activist for many decades. Graca was an excellent student in her early school days, which made her win a place at Lisbon University in Portugal- an honor that few women had achieved. Those were the times when Mozambique was still a colony of Portugal. Students studying abroad put together an underground liberation movement, FRELIMO, to fight for Independence in Mozambique, and Graça joined the movement. After overthrowing the fascist government, Mozambique gained independence, and FRELIMO became the interim government.

At 29 years, Graca became FRELIMO's secretary of education. At that time, Samora Machel became the president of Mozambique after being a champion of the liberation struggle. Graça got married to Samora Machel, and she was an important government figure holding a ministry in education. The main goal of Graça in FRELIMO was a socialist goal of achieving universal education for all. The Portuguese rulership left a colonial illiteracy legacy, which made Graça's task monumental.

In three years of leadership, Graca saw the enrollment of 700,000 children in primary school. After a decade, the number of students in primary and secondary schools rose from 40% to 90%

for males and 75% for females. The war of destabilization in Mozambique from 1977, where the anti-FRELIMO army called RENAMO targeted schools and health clinics, saw over 45% of the primary school network and 490 health centers destroyed. When Samora Machel's presidential jet crashed mysteriously just inside the South African border, Graça and many other people of Mozambique believed South African agents killed him because of Samora's policy of giving ANC- members of the outlawed South African movement ANC sanctuary on Mozambique soil. When her husband died, Graça said, *"They believe that if they cut down the tallest trees, they can destroy the forest."* Graca intensified her commitment to developing and expanding her efforts on behalf of children everywhere.

When the war ended in 1992, Graça kept working to rehabilitate the over 1.5 million refugees. Additionally, she began developing ways to empower the women of Mozambique and undo the damage the war had inflicted on children. She later became the chairperson of the National Organization of Children of Mozambique. She was determined to understand why "there are societies which deliberately target children by killing them, torturing them and making them part of the destructive process—like in Rwanda and Mozambique."

U.N. organizations like UNICEF partnered with her and she became a Goodwill Ambassador. She also started her Foundation for Communal Work. Graça addresses the emotional needs of people suffering silently due to the effects of war for years afterwards, and many young people cynically exploited as combatants. Her concern with rapid social change and the breakdown of the family has prompted Graça to ask Africans to "decolonize" their minds and encourage their young people to have pride in being African. She states, "*As Africans, we can be impoverished, but we are not poor. ... We have the learning capacity to learn from others, but we also have a lot to offer the world.*"

3. Angelina Jolie

Many have cherished the progress of this talented American actress, humanitarian and filmmaker. The successful career, wealth and milestones in the Hollywood world have not stopped the 46-year-old Oscar-winning actress from being a down-to-earth quality individual who is blessed with a rare emotional intelligence that ranks her top in the industry. Angelina Jolie uses her stardom for a meaningful cause that benefits the least fortunate, unlike many other famous movie stars. Not all celebs are simultaneously known to be top Hollywood actresses and humanitarian workers, but Angelina Jolie can boast of both. The star has been a Special Envoy with the United Nations High Commissioner for Refugees (UNHCR) since 2012. She was a Goodwill Ambassador for the same organization from 2001 to 2012. During an interview with *Vogue* on her humanitarian work, she said she found herself a student at these organizations' "feet," where she learned more from refugees about family, dignity, resilience, and survival. Despite being able to afford a life of luxury and comfort, she goes out on field missions to crisis zones because she sees all people as equal. She told Vogue that she sees the abuse and suffering and cannot stand by. Jolie states, "*Around the world, many people are running away from gas attacks, rape, beatings, female genital mutilation, persecution and murder. They flee to survive and improve their lives. I want to see an end to anything that forces people out of their homelands.*"

Angelina Jolie says her determination was further propelled when she cried as she listened to refugees' stories during a mission in Sierra Leone. She recalls an amazing grandmother who was looking after her orphaned grandkids. The grandmother pulled her up and told her not to cry but to help. That was always her motivation.

Another thing that influences Jolie's humanitarian work is motherhood. When she was on a mission in Cambodia in 2001, she came across a little boy in an orphanage, who she later adopted and named Maddox. In Cambodia, she began to engage in foreign affairs like never before and joined UNHCR, apart from making her a mom. She went ahead to build a home in Cambodia, where she set up the headquarters for her foundation there. In November 2006, Jolie expanded the scope of her foundation, renamed the Maddox Jolie-Pitt Foundation (MJP) to create Asia's first Millennium Village, following U.N. development goals. A meeting with the founder of Millennium Promise, notable economist Jeffrey Sachs, at the World Economic Forum, where she was an invited speaker in two years, 2005 and 2006 inspired her. Together with Jeffery, they filmed a 2005 MTV special podcast, *The Diary of Angelina Jolie & Dr. Jeffrey Sachs,* in western Africa, which followed them on a trip to a Millennium Village in western Kenya.

By mid-2007, some 6,000 villagers and 72 employees, some former poachers employed as rangers, lived and worked at MJP in ten villages that were previously isolated from one another. Its compound included schools, roads, and a milk factory funded by Jolie. Her home acted as the MJP field headquarters. In her remarks at one red carpet function, Jolie said, *"there is nothing more beautiful, challenging and unsettling than the free mind of a thinking woman. That is why effort is put into constraining women."* All these efforts portray her emotional empowerment to many, and this gave power of speech to women all over the world.

4. Michelle Obama

Who could ever imagine a black woman becoming the first African-American First Lady of the United States of America? Through her four main initiatives, Michelle has become a role model for women and an advocate for a healthy community, service members and their families, and international adolescent girls' education. Through this, she was able to depict the emotional empowerment of women.

After a few years, Michelle Obama decided her true calling was working with people to serve their communities and neighbors. She served as the assistant commissioner of planning and development in Chicago City Hall before becoming the founding executive manager of the Chicago chapter of Public Allies. This AmeriCorps program prepares youth for public service. In 2010, she launched *Let's Move!* The initiative brings together community leaders, educators, medical professionals, parents, and others nationwide to address the challenge of childhood obesity. *Let's Move!* The initiative has an ambitious goal: to solve the epidemic of childhood obesity within a generation that showed her emotional empowerment of women. Whether it's providing food in our schools or helping kids be more active, or urging companies to advertise healthier foods to our children, *Let's Move!* It is focused on giving parents the support they need to make healthier choices for their kids.

Mitchelle Obama has continued her efforts to support and inspire young people during her time as First Lady. In 2014, Michelle Obama launched the *Reach Higher Initiative* to inspire young people across America to take ownership of their future by completing their education at the highest level possible, whether at a professional training program, a college or a university. *Reach Higher* aims to ensure that all children and learners understand what they need to excel in their education by working to expose students to college, helping them understand financial knowledge eligibility, encouraging academic and summer learning opportunities, and supporting school counsellors who do essential work to help students get into college.

In 2015, Michelle Obama joined President Obama in launching *Let Girls Learn*. This U.S. government initiative was to help girls worldwide go to school and stay in school. As part of this effort, Michelle Obama is calling on states across the globe to help educate and empower all women. She is sharing the stories and struggles of these women with the world here at home to inspire them to be determined in their education. During her last speech on a climate of fear, uncertainty and divisiveness, she told young people: *"Don't be afraid. Be focused. Be determined. Be hopeful. Be empowered."*

In her continued quest to admonish fear, Mitchelle focused her audience's attention on how much each mattered, urging all the young people to be focused and determined. She also went ahead, calling for people to live in hope rather than fear and to believe in their value, which is powerful on its own, but she didn't stop there. She called on her audience to work hard to protect the freedoms they enjoyed. In one of her speeches,

Michelle Obama had a plea for empowerment which she framed in the context of education, urging everyone to empower themselves with good education and use it to build a country worth boundless promise.

5. Oprah Winfrey

It is said that anyone who has ever struggled with poverty knows how expensive it is to be poor. Winfrey was born in poverty in a rural state in the Southeastern United States to a single teenage mother and later raised in the inner city. Oprah was defiled by her uncle, cousin and family friend during her early childhood; during this period, she never expected to be a mother. After years of abuse, at 13, she decided to run away from home, and at 14, she became pregnant. However, her son, who was born prematurely, died in infancy. Oprah felt betrayed by a family member who sold the story of her son to the National Enquirer. Winfrey's first job as a young girl was working at a local grocery, and at the age of 17, she won the Miss Black Tennessee beauty pageant. With that, she attracted the attention of the local black radio stations.

Winfrey landed a job at WVOL, a radio station serving the Nashville African American community. While she was in high school and at 19, she was a co-anchor for the local evening news. Winfrey was often emotional, and because of her spontaneous delivery, she was transferred to the daytime talk show arena. She boosted the local talk show to first place and later launched her own production company. Winfrey relocated to her hometown Chicago to host WLS-TV's low-rated half-hour morning talk show after being hired there, and within a few months of taking over, the show increased from last place in the ratings and was ranked the first talk show in Chicago.

Aside from her talk show, Winfrey produced and co-starred in the drama miniseries The Women of Brewster Place and its short-lived Brewster Place. As well as hosting television shows, Winfrey founded the women's cable T.V. network, which was the initial network for *Winfrey Oprah After The Show* from 2002 to 2006 before moving to her firm, when Winfrey sold her stake in the network.

Winfrey hosted a prime-time interview with Michael Jackson, which was among the fourth most-watched event in American television history and the most-watched interview ever. Winfrey has authored five books. At the announcement of a weight loss book in 2005, co-authored with her trainer Bob Greene, her undisclosed advance fee had broken the record for the world's highest book fee, previously held by the autobiography of former U.S. President Bill Clinton. Winfrey's company created a website to provide resources and interactive content related to her shows, book club, and public charity.

Oprah.com had more than 70 million views and more than six million monthly users and received approximately 20,000 weekly e-mails. Through her show and website, Winfrey initiated "Oprah's Child Predator Watch List" to help track down accused child molesters. Within 48 hours, two of the featured men were captured. Oprah is an inspiration of emotional empowerment overcoming the worst experiences a woman can go through of sexual abuse.

6. Naomi Osaka

Naomi Osaka is one of the excellent tennis players. At 23, she was already the greatest tennis player in the world. With such achievement, it seemed easy for her to be silent, rest on her accolades, and rely on being young and gifted. However, the thing is, she's Black. Black excellence always comes with responsibility, and being young, gifted and Black meant using her platform for protest. Despite the racial challenges, she rose to the game by beating Serena Williams in the tennis game to nab her first Grand Slam title. This was in a sport overshadowed by racism and sexism. As she rose in the ranks, the world paid closer attention, commenting on her every move on the court. When she became the player to beat, the stress started weighing her down, affecting her game and her feelings of self-worth. It was even more painful when she lost because of the endless questions from the media.

She had to respond to media questions about why she was unable to do the one thing she had been training since birth to do: win. Osaka withdrew from the French Open tennis tournament after announcing that she would not do the official press events, which led to controversy. Osaka was brave enough to admit the reason for her withdrawal in 28 words as part of the larger statement on Twitter. She says, *"The truth remains I have suffered long bouts of depression in the U.S. Open since 2018 and I have had a really hard time coping with that."* Osaka's admissions of emotional drain took bravery to share this message with the world.

But in doing so, she created a powerful and emotional bridge that saw her fans empathize with her and elevated both her and the audience that believed in her. That's a sign of emotional intelligence.

Reflections

1. Do you know any woman who you believe to be emotionally empowered?
2. What character traits do you admire in her or think make her qualify as emotionally empowered?
3. Have you experienced infidelity or betrayal in your relationship? Did you stay, or did you leave?
4. Do you consider yourself emotionally empowered because of the decision you've made?

Final Take Away

From the illustrations of these prestigious women, their emotional empowerment has indeed benefitted the community in many ways. The likes of Graca Machel, who kept going despite the mysterious death of her husband to help women and children, go to schools, and Angelina Jolie, whose emotional empowerment led her to help many families in impoverished countries. Most of all we see 2 women- the former first lady Michelle Obama and Ophrah Winfrey rise to prominence against all odds. Indeed, emotional empowerment is a Win-Win for us and the world! Bravo to these role models.

CHAPTER 4:

STEVEN COVEY'S TAKE ON EMOTIONS

Stephen Covey's best-seller book, "The 7 Habits of Highly Effective People" can help people achieve success both professionally and personally. By incorporating the seven habits into our lives, women can begin to change the way they think about themselves and how to manage emotions for better relationships with others. Get these golden nuggets in this chapter.

How The 7 Habits of Highly Effective People affect Emotions

Stephen Covey's book, *"The 7 Habits of Highly Effective People"* uses a principle-centred approach for personal and interpersonal effectiveness. This is meant to cope with one's inner character or motives rather than the outward look of your behaviour. Emotional empowerment is not something that happens overnight; it takes time and practice. But by following the principles set out in *"The 7 Habits of Highly Effective People,"* we can slowly but surely build up our confidence and take control of our lives. Here are the ways the 7 habits can help you become more emotionally empowered.

Habit 1: Be proactive

The term proactive means taking good responsibility for your life. Reactive people are driven by their feelings, but assertive people are guided by the values they own. Proactive women will focus on things they have control over. Reactive women conversely concentrate on things they have no power over which leads to wasting time and energy and increased unhappiness.

Habit 2: Think of the end in mind

Convey elaborates that the most effective way to start with the end in mind is by creating personal mission statements that focus on character, contributions and achievements and associated values. These values will help women to control their emotions by prioritizing their focus on spending emotional energy on more important things like building relationships and achieving their goals. This will lead to higher emotional empowerment.

Habit 3: Putting first things first

When we focus on tasks that are meaningful to our vision for the future, we can put our energy into things that hold value. For women, it's especially beneficial as prioritization requires us to examine our values and bring them into the decisions that guide our personal and professional lives. With clear priorities in place, a woman can free her time, energy, and resources for meaningful projects that drive her toward her dreams. All this contributes to greater emotional empowerment and resiliency - allowing women to rise above life's obstacles.

Habit 4: Think win-win.

This is a philosophy of human interaction and not techniques, as Convey argues. This means that all agreements are equally beneficial, and all parties will feel satisfied with the outcome. When supporting this mindset, life should be considered cooperation, not competition. Therefore, for a woman to adopt a win-win attitude, she must cultivate the habit of interpersonal leadership, which involves becoming self-aware, becoming an independent thinker, empathetic, a good listener and communicative. This will help her emotional state when socializing with other people.

Habit 5: Seeking first to understand, then to be understood

A woman will become a proficient listener who will listen with the intent to understand and be understood. Through this, a woman will gain the skill of empathic listening, thus empowering her emotionally. This allows women to get a clear picture of reality.

Since the woman is an emphatic listener, she can communicate ideas and meet the listener's concerns. This will increase the credibility of her thoughts when speaking to the audience.

Habit 6: Synergize

Synergy is a powerful tool for women's emotional empowerment. When we synergize – that is, when we come together with other individuals to share our ideas, aspirations, and experiences – we open ourselves up to the richness of our collective potential. Working in a supportive environment allows us to be seen, heard, as well as to receive and learn from each other.

With this sense of collaboration come enhanced self-awareness, increased accountability, and greater creativeness that further help fuel personal successes. Synergizing allows us to build positive energy around common goals, summon up courage from within to face life's challenges and nurture our emotional wellness with understanding, respect and fellowship.

Habit 7: Sharpen the Saw

This involves using the energy we have effectively and sustainably rather than burning out by trying to do too much through taking regular breaks from work - for example, engaging in activities that restore us and make us feel more energized. The 4 areas of renewal are physical, social/emotional, mental, and spiritual. We can therefore keep our mental faculties sharp and avoid physically and mentally draining ourselves. We can also strive for a balanced lifestyle by making sure that we take time away from our hectic lives to connect with friends and family. Achieving this balance will help us develop creative solutions during problem-solving situations and provide mental clarity throughout our daily actions. Taking a step back, being mindful of ourselves, and simply allowing ourselves some space to breathe are all essential aspects of honing in on one's emotional power.

Reflections

1. *How many of these skills do you practice and apply on a scale of 0-10?*
2. *Identify 1 action you can take to practice and develop more of these habits.*
3. *How much more emotionally empowered could you be in you practiced 80% of these habits?*

Final Take Away

By practicing these 7 habits of highly effective people, you will see a greater resiliency, patience and understanding of yourself and others. These habits will help develop your emotional empowerment. Start using them today!

PART 3:

HOW TO BE AN EMOTIONALLY EMPOWERED WOMAN

CHAPTER 1:

EMOTIONAL SELF-CARE

This chapter is designed to help women who are ready to embrace their emotions and get to the next level. We will discover why emotional self-care is key to rising above the emotional stigma women face and gaining emotional empowerment.

What is Emotional Self-Care?

Self-care is defined as everything you do to look out for yourself to keep physically, intellectually, and emotionally well. This is the intentional practice of taking action to maintain or improve one's health, well-being, and happiness, particularly during difficult circumstances. Various types of self-care improve physical, mental, and emotional health, resulting in a broad sense of well-being. We may use emotional self-care to improve our health and well-being by working with our emotions. It is a technique for establishing control over who we are, recognizing, feeling, caring for ourselves, and devoting time to our thoughts and emotions. Emotional self-care comprises becoming aware of and understanding one's feelings and allowing oneself to lean into them to honor oneself and one's emotions. We can attempt to ignore, reject, or conceal our emotions, but they will inevitably come to light.

Women should also remember that self-care does not indicate self-indulgence or selfishness, but rather taking care of yourself to stay well, perform your work, help and respect others, and achieve everything you need and want to do in a day. Women should not think of self-care as a one-time indulgence but rather as a long-term practice to promote resilience, health, and well-being. We are more likely to observe gains in our life when we take care of ourselves, such as our physical health, relationships, self-esteem, and stress management. Women must note that self-care is not a "one-size-fits-all" activity; instead, they must develop personalized self-care regimens based on their requirements. There is no set rule for when or how to do it, but doing something for yourself every day starts a positive habit.

Why You Need to Practice Emotional Self-Care

Stress and busy schedules can take a toll on our mental health, making us feel drained, anxious, and overwhelmed. Self-care is an essential component for maintaining emotional intelligence and overall well-being.

1. It helps us let go of stress and negative energy

Taking time out to invest in ourselves can help clear the mental clutter that prevents us from effectively managing our emotions and relationships. From carving out a few moments for daily meditation or yoga practice to scheduling regular massage appointments and eating healthy meals, self-care activities provide the necessary space to decompress.

2. It helps us develop compassion for ourselves and others

Furthermore, investing in our own well-being helps us show more patience towards others, become better listeners, and be kinder to ourselves when we make mistakes. Ultimately, by caring for our minds and bodies through self-care, we create a better environment for our emotional lives — allowing us to live with greater compassion, peace of mind, and understanding of ourselves and others around us.

3. You're able to deal with challenges

When you have a healthy attitude about your feelings and how to express them, you are better equipped to deal with situations rather than feeling overwhelmed and incapable of dealing with the issue each time a powerful emotion strikes. Ideally, your feelings should help you understand what is happening.

How to Practice Emotional Self-Care

1. Make Time

To have a good self-care regime, you may start by attending to your emotional needs by scheduling time for things that make you joyful and healthily managing your stress.

2. Communicate your feelings

It also requires learning to effectively articulate your feelings, which you may do by journaling and communicating with others who empower and support you.

3. **Start small**

Experts recommend starting small rather than tackling the most challenging thing first to get into a habit of regularly practicing self-care. Choose one practice to incorporate into your daily routine each week. Keep track of any positive changes and add more exercises as you feel ready.

4. **Practice any of these activities during your self-care time**

   - Be Mindful of what you feel in that moment
   - Consciously choose how to respond to tough situations
   - Practice gratitude
   - Stay connected to supportive relationships
   - Limit your exposure to negative news
   - Practice meditation
   - Move your body with exercise or dancing
   - Laugh!
   - Take up a relaxing hobby

With regular practice you will start to feel better and more in control of your emotions.

Reflections

1. *Do you think it is vital for women to practice self-care? Why?*
2. *Do you practice self-care?*
3. *Would you like to start a routine or enhance an existing one?*
4. *What would you include in the routine?*
5. *Create a self-care routine plan and follow through for the next one week, record the activities you did and reward yourself for the gains, improve on the fails.*

Final Take Away

Emotional self-care is critical to the emotional well-being of a woman. Make sure you take time for yourself every day – even if it's just 10 minutes, to do something calming and relaxing that makes you happy. If you're struggling emotionally and don't know where to start with self-care, talk to your doctor, contact a therapist, look into local support groups or reach out to one of the many online communities dedicated to helping women thrive emotionally!

CHAPTER 2:

BEING EMOTIONALLY EMPOWERED

There's no doubt that as women, we are constantly juggling a lot of different responsibilities and roles. But we mustn't lose sight of our own needs along the way. This chapter will reveal how to claim emotional empowerment for better happier lives.

To effectively empower a woman, a double-edged sword action plan is required. Both society and the woman must collaborate to achieve this goal. The first step is to understand what it means to be an empowered woman and, more importantly, how to become one.

Who Is the Emotionally Empowered Woman?

The Cambridge Dictionary defines empowerment as "giving someone or a party the official authority or the freedom to do something." Female empowerment, therefore, refers to the realization, both individually and collectively, that women can be the owners of their actions, act, and ultimately lead their lives.

An emotionally empowered individual has mastered their emotions with deep understanding and can use that to their advantage. The ability to manage and control one's feelings, be assertive and purposeful with one's emotions, and be confident and intentional with the choices one makes are some notable traits of an emotionally empowered individual.

The Beca's Santander women scholarships define empowered women as having the following characteristics:

1. **They develop their unique leadership style.**

It doesn't necessarily mean following the footsteps of traditionally male leaders. Empowered women are professionals who can find their way to inspire and motivate others. Their presence always makes an impact as empowered women know what they're about, are confident in what they want, and strive to achieve their goals.

2. **They wield considerable power.**

The empowered woman has an impact on her surroundings. Her warm, approachable personality makes it easy for people to engage and be around her. She not only possesses the professional skills to forge her path, but she also possesses the necessary attitude to spread her empowerment at all levels and become a reference.

3. **They are enthusiastic about new ideas.**

To obtain this support, empowered women take on the responsibility of effecting change, departing from the traditional role that society has assigned them, and exploring innovative paths, both in their acting style and their work projects.

4. **They advocate for female empowerment.**

Knowing the circumstances and obstacles that many working women face, empowered women do not seek to compete or compare themselves to others but instead fight to remove those barriers and invite other professionals to follow in their footsteps.

5. **They understand the art of communication, negotiation, and persuasion.**

These are the key abilities that stand out as female empowerment leadership skills. The empowered woman can share her message and understand herself as she is articulate and concise in conveying emotions to her audience. She can soberly take criticism or correction positively.

How to Be More Emotionally Empowered

By understanding and managing emotions, women may break away from their emotional labels and preconceptions and achieve incredible success in all parts of their lives. Emotionally empowered women exhibit strength, confidence, and excellent control of their emotions. They recognize that their emotions are a vital tool for personal growth and accomplishment. To get started on your path to emotional health, this is what you must do:

1. **Find A Sound Support System**

Many people believe that being self-sufficient is better, and their health is a personal concern. While doing certain things on your own is necessary, having a support system for you when things go rough is crucial to sustaining your emotional health and maintaining emotional balance.

A support system comprises a person or group of persons you may rely on for mutual emotional assistance, where both parties will perform the role of a listener at some point. It represents a person or group demonstrating empathy, love, and trust. This system could consist of a group of friends, family members, or a therapist and having people you can rely on to support you through tough times

Support systems provide increased well-being, improved coping abilities, and a longer, healthier life. It also helps alleviate depression, anxiety, and stress. We all require a support system to flourish.

When interacting with others in your support, it is critical to provide cues to help them understand how you are feeling. These cues could include emotional expression through body language, such as various facial expressions associated with the specific emotions you are experiencing. In other cases, it may entail stating your feelings directly. When you tell friends or family members that you are happy, sad, excited, or scared, you are providing them with vital information that they can use to take appropriate action. If you feel like you're struggling with your emotional health, it is also a good idea to seek professional help. A therapist or coach can help you understand and manage your emotions healthily.

Most of us do not receive the emotional training required to experience and express our emotions healthily and productively. We can go through the ups and downs of life much more successfully when we have emotional support and we realize that we don't have to do it alone. It is acceptable and crucial for us to seek and receive assistance. To make significant progress in developing yourself or learning new abilities, you must surround yourself with the proper people. You want the appropriate people to be there to support and encourage you as you travel through life.

How to Find a Support System

1. Be willing to ask for help when you need it and take it as gracefully as possible. Participate in a new group or individual activities to meet new people who can be a beneficial influence. Consider joining a sports team or a fitness group to enhance your mood, improve your physical health, and allow you to socialize with others.
2. Examine your present social groups and family ties, and identify the people who provide the most positive yet honest advice. Social assistance provides a link to the outside world while allowing you to focus on other people and interactions. It can sometimes take the shape of a heart-to-heart with a friend and the pursuit of beneficial advice. You may also receive some guidance since a support system is mutually beneficial and everyone is an expert in one or more areas.
3. Join online support groups that bring together people who have had similar experiences and comprise people who have shared experiences serving our emotional needs. The group should allow participants to discuss their experiences, thoughts, coping skills, or direct knowledge

about diseases or treatments. They could be face-to-face meetings, teleconferences, and online communities guided by a layperson or a professional facilitator.

Reflections

- *Do you believe a support system is essential to developing your emotional health?*
- *Who can you identify as your support system?*
- *What do they contribute to your emotional health journey?*
- *Is seeking professional help a good move for you?*

2. Develop A Healthy Coping Mechanism

Coping skills assist you in tolerating, minimizing, and dealing with stressful circumstances in your life. Stress management may help you feel better physically and mentally, and it can influence your capacity to perform at your best. Make sure you're taking care of yourself by getting enough sleep, eating a healthy diet, and getting regular exercise.

When you're feeling stressed or upset, it's essential to have healthy ways to deal with those emotions, including journaling, deep breathing exercises, or talking to a friend. However, not all coping mechanisms are equal. In trying to cope, it might be tempting to indulge in tactics that provide immediate relief but may cause you more trouble in the long run. Ultimately, make sure you are taking time for yourself to do things that make you happy.

Reflections

- *Are you tempted to seek remedies that provide immediate relief in stressful situations?*
- *What is your go-to coping mechanism?*

1. **Accept your Feelings as Valid**

Many people find it difficult to admit that their feelings are just as essential as anybody else's. They worry that their feelings and wants aren't as vital as other people's. They believe that acknowledging their emotions is selfish, self-absorbed, and even arrogant.

Some of us do not regard ourselves authentically enough to recognize that our emotions also matter. Many of us believe that we do not deserve certain things, making us feel and express certain feelings uncomfortably.

Furthermore, we are frequently trained to prioritize other people's needs and feelings over our own. We are not taught appropriate methods that help acknowledge our emotions, which leads us to assume that our sentiments are unimportant.

It's humbling to realize that it isn't and appreciate the significance of recognizing that all sentiments count. It's about being true to ourselves, being honest about how we feel and what we want, and participating in genuine dialogues with others, even if we don't feel or desire the same things they do.

Reflections

- *Do you believe that it's okay to feel sad, angry, or scared?*
- *How important is it to acknowledge and accept your feelings rather than trying to bury them?*

- *Do you find it difficult to admit that our emotions are essential for various reasons?*
- *Does your concern about what other people think of you hold you back?*
- *Are you afraid that others will not like, approve, or comprehend your feelings?*
- *Make a concerted effort to improve your self-esteem.*

2. Build your Low Self-Esteem

Your present levels of self-confidence and balance are the outcome of what you have encountered in your life, and they have a significant influence on every part of life that contributes to well-being. Low self-esteem causes much pain since many people look down on themselves and undervalue themselves. Some people believe that having poor self-esteem is an irreversible element of their nature.

People with low self-esteem have emotions of guilt, self-doubt, and inadequacy, which impede them from having happy relationships or pursuing their aspirations.

The unfortunate truth about a woman's self-worth is that her body image heavily influences it. Remember the phrase "I believe, therefore I am." Concentrate on your cognitive abilities rather than your external characteristics.

Increasing one's self-esteem can be a time-consuming process. Overcoming established mindsets and habits generally needs much effort. Elizabeth Cush, MA, LCPC, says that "*Learning new things takes time. When attempting to improve self-esteem, practice and patience are required.*"

One way to improve your self-esteem is to learn more about yourself -your strengths and weaknesses. By focusing on your strengths, and minimizing weaknesses, you can acquire new skills that will prepare you to face new professional stages and you can redefine your limits.

3. Take care of your physical well-being

Taking care of your physical well-being plays an important role in emotional empowerment. Experiencing good health means more energy and less stress, while "feel-good hormones" are released when engaging in physical activities or eating nutritious foods - leading to increased self-confidence and positivity throughout the day. The culmination of good food and a healthy body will enable you to believe in yourself more when asserting your goals and beliefs.

4. Be assertive and stand up for yourself and your beliefs.

Being assertive is a key factor in feeling empowered as a woman; by speaking up for what you believe in, even if it means facing criticism or pushback, you will create a foundation for feeling strong enough to take risks and make tough decisions.

5. Improve your communication skills.

Improving communication skills can help you navigate personal relationships more confidently - from asking for help from friends to voicing personal concerns. This enables women to have productive conversations without fear or hesitation.

6. Journal Regularly

Finding ways to express your feelings, even on paper, is very therapeutic. This process also helps you to learn how to communicate your feelings and speak with people in a more empowered way.

7. Set short-term and long-term objectives.

Overly ambitious goals risk draining your motivation and willpower because they are more complex and time-consuming. What steps can you take to avoid this? In addition to setting long-term goals, break them down into small milestones that you can conquer one at a time. As you accomplish the smaller tasks, your self-confidence and emotional belief in yourself will increase.

8. Step outside of your comfort zone.

A strong woman is not afraid to face new challenges. When you have the opportunity, get out of your comfort zone and see how you conquer your fears and gain new experiences that will help you open many doors and value yourself more and more. Also, before rejecting or not interacting with toxic people, you maintain a balance that of peace which allows you to thrive in what you truly want.

9. Search for opportunities to learn and grow from every situation.

Seek to learn and grow from every event. Also seek opportunities and actions that lead toward self-improvement. Analyzing your thoughts helps you to shift your attention from difficulties to opportunities. When you've discovered opportunities, act by taking the necessary actions to improve your emotional state. For example, a bad experience can teach you how not to respond the next time you feel that way.

10. Be True to Yourself.

It's okay to seek inspiration or support, but don't forget to be authentic and guided by your values and purposes. You will only be able to progress on this path if you believe in your goals and act independently.

Reflections

- *How important is it to have balanced self-esteem?*
- *Do you have low or balanced self-esteem?*
- *Have you gone through the transition from low to high self-esteem?*
- *Do you believe that developing self-worth takes time?*
- *What steps should one take to build self-esteem?*
- *How important is emotional balance to you?*
- *Do you have goals for your emotional health and balance?*
- *What measures will you take to be more emotionally balanced?*

Final Take Away

By building these twelve components, women can advance emotionally toward greater comfort, autonomy, and respect. With each step taken towards improving the quality of one's life comes the hope that eventually, a woman can see the world through a lens free of self-doubt and external bias. Fostering emotional empowerment is possible if one invests time in honing these twelve essential actions.

CHAPTER 3:

COMMUNICATION AND EMOTIONAL EMPOWERMENT OF WOMEN

Communication is key for expressing your emotions, exchange of ideas and the peaceful resolution of conflicts. In this chapter, we shall look at ways to communicate in a way that builds you emotionally.

What is Effective Communication?

There is more to communicating than just sharing facts. That's why it's crucial to grasp the motivations and feelings of everyone involved. It is not enough to simply articulate your thoughts; you must also be able to listen to others in a way that allows you to fully get what they are saying and leaves them feeling heard and understood.

Common Barriers to Effective Communication

1. **Tension and irrational feelings.**

Misreading other people, sending nonverbal cues that are ambiguous or off-putting, and reverting to bad habits are all more likely when you're feeling worried or emotionally overwhelmed. You can teach yourself to take a deep breath and center yourself before resuming a discussion to reduce the likelihood of arguments and misunderstandings.

2. Lack of Focus.

Inefficient communication is a direct result of juggling too many tasks at once. It's likely, you won't pick up on nonverbal signs in a discussion if you're checking your phone, thinking about what you'll say next, or daydreaming. To get your point over, you need to concentrate without interruptions.

3. Inconsistent Body Language.

What is being stated should be supported by nonverbal cues, not undermined. It's easy to be seen as dishonest if what you say conflicts with your body language. For example, saying yes and shaking your head can't go together.

4. Distressing Nonverbal Cues.

Crossing your arms, avoiding eye contact, and tapping your feet are all examples of negative body language that can be used to communicate that you disagree with or detest what is being stated. Even if you don't agree with or appreciate what's being said, it's crucial to avoid sending negative signals and to communicate clearly, and not put the other person on the defensive.

Effective Ways of Communicating Emotions

1. Be an Engaged Listener

What we should say is a common point of concentration in any conversation. However, listening is more important than talking when communicating effectively. One of the keys to effective listening is picking up on the speaker's tone of voice as well as their intended meaning. Taking the time to listen instead of just hearing makes a huge impact. If you listen attentively, you'll pick up on the nuances in a person's tone of voice that reveal their state of mind and the feelings they're trying to convey.

2. Be Attentive to the Non-verbal Cues

Words alone may not fully express how I feel, but how I look, listen, move, and react to others certainly can. Facial expressions, physical movements and gestures, eye contact, posture, vocal tone, muscular tension and respiration are all examples of nonverbal communication. You can improve your social life, relationships at home and work, your capacity to handle stressful situations, and your success in general by working on your ability to read and apply nonverbal cues.

3. Learn to Keep Stress in Check

How often have you been anxious and said or done something you subsequently regretted during an argument with your partner, children, superior, friends, or colleagues? If you can immediately calm yourself down, you can avoid regrets like these, and, in many circumstances, you can even assist the other person in relaxing. You can't tell if the scenario calls for a response or if the other person's signals signify that it would be better not to talk until you're completely relaxed and serene. Emotional control, quick thinking, and clear communication are necessary for high-stakes scenarios like a job interview, business presentation, high-pressure meeting, or introduction to a loved one's family.

4. Maintain composure in high-stakes conversations.

This is the best way to manage your emotions and communicate in a high-emotion situation.

- **Use delay techniques to buy some mental processing time.**
  If you are not sure how to answer a statement or question, simply ask for clarification.

- **Take a minute to gather your thoughts.**
  Gathering your thoughts before responding gives the impression that you have everything under control, so don't be afraid to be silent.

- **Focus on a single point and back it up with evidence.**
  A lengthy response or one that flits from topic-to-topic risks losing the attention of the person listening to you. If you want to know if your audience is still with you after making a point, give them an example to illustrate it.

- **Give precise instructions.**
  Often, the delivery of a message is just as crucial as the message itself. Make eye contact, speak in a calm, steady tone, and avoid mumbling.

- **Conclude by summarizing what you just said.**
  Stop talking after you've summarized your response; everyone will be OK. To avoid awkwardness, you need

not continue talking when there is a pause in the conversation.

5. Assert Yourself

Expressing yourself confidently and directly improves your communication, self-image, and decision-making ability. To be assertive is to speak up for oneself and others while maintaining a healthy balance between the two. It has nothing to do with being disagreeable or demanding. Never try to convince someone of your point of view or win an argument at the expense of your listeners.

How to Become More Assertive

1. Respect yourself and value your choices. They should be given the same weight as those of everyone else.
2. Identify your wants and needs. Master expressing your views without violating the rights of others.
3. Positively communicate your negative feelings. Even if you're furious, you should treat the other person respectfully.
4. Positively receive feedback. Be humble when complimented, reflective when making mistakes, and resourceful when seeking assistance.
5. Find your "no" voice. Don't allow people to push you beyond your comfort zone. Find other solutions so that everyone can be satisfied with the result.

Learning To Express Yourself Confidently

1. Care for the other person is communicated by assertiveness that shows empathy.
2. Recognize the other person's feelings and experiences before expressing your own. For example, you can use this approach, *"I appreciate your hard work, but please don't forget we are in this team together."*
3. If your initial assertions are ineffective, you can try raising the stakes. Your demands get more specific and dire as time goes on, and you may even threaten action if ignored. For instance: *"I will have to take legal action if you violate the terms of the contract."*

Quick Stress Relief to Communicate Effectively

When the temperature of a conversation rises, you need a quick and effective way to cool things down before things get out of hand. You may safely take stock of whatever intense emotions you're feeling, manage your sentiments, and act appropriately if you know how to relieve stress quickly.

1. **Learn to identify the signs of a growing sense of stress.**

Your body will let you know if you're under too much pressure during the conversation. Is your stomach or muscles knotted up? Do you have fists that you're clenching? Do you have shallow breathing? Do you feel like you're "forgetting to breathe?"

2. **Wait until you've calmed down**

Do this before determining whether or not to continue a conversation.

3. **Try to find the funny side of the situation.**

In a conversation, comedy may be a terrific stress reliever if used correctly. Whenever you or others around you begin to take things too seriously, try telling a joke or relating a funny anecdote to bring everyone back to a more relaxed state of mind.

4. **Maintain a sense of flexibility.**

If both parties are willing to bend a little, a satisfactory compromise can be reached that alleviates tension for everyone involved. Understanding that the other person places a higher value on a certain topic than you might make reaching a compromise easier and more worthwhile.

When Is Communication Critical for Emotional Empowerment?

Circumstances when you need communication to protect your emotional and mental health and empower yourself are;

1. **When Setting Boundaries**

Boundaries have an impact on every aspect of our lives: Physical boundaries help us determine who may touch us and under what conditions; mental limits allow us to have our thoughts and opinions; and emotional boundaries allow us to deal with our own emotions while disengaging from the harmful, manipulative emotions of others. Spiritual boundaries assist us in distinguishing God's will from our own, and they renew our awe for our Creator. A healthy, emotionally balanced lifestyle necessitates the establishment of clear boundaries.

Healthy boundaries are essential for self-care. We feel depleted, taken advantage of, taken for granted, or intruded upon when no limits exist. At the same time, poor boundaries in any relationship may lead to resentment, hurt, anger, and burnout. When setting boundaries, we must never forget that boundaries necessitate two (2) limits: limits set on others and ourselves.

In her article on *Living Well and Loving your Life*, Sharon Martins suggests an identified format for setting boundaries that encourage women to:

1. Set limits for their well-being rather than exert control over others.
2. Recognize that boundary setting is a continuous process rather than a one-time event. Therefore, they will accept failures and any lapses that arise and adjust as they go.
3. Be direct and do not apologize for their requirements to avoid retrogressing.
4. Expect opposition, but not let it deter them; resistance may lead to guilt trips that lead to apologizing and consequent retrogression as they give the opposition an edge.
5. Be specific about what they want and why they want it. Being clear enables them to be firm in execution and aids in open communication with the opponent.

Women Can Accomplish This By:

1. Stating the boundary clearly and concisely.

For example, if you told someone, *"I would like/appreciate it if you could ask first before picking up my belongings."*

This statement expressly informs the other party that:

1. You are dissatisfied with how they take your belongings without permission
2. They are required to ask before taking your belongings from that point forward.

2. Communicate your needs and avoid focusing on others.

This means that you must express your needs without implying your expectations of others' behaviour.

For instance, you should say, *"I would appreciate some peace while studying"* versus *"I would greatly appreciate it if you stopped making noise during my study time."*

3. Avoid the Ego state of overexplaining

Resist the urge to explain because the ego will always seek to defend. Rather than attempting to control the other person, a simple no, and a boundary will allow them to choose their response.

4. Declare your follow-through

This is how you will react and follow through if someone crosses the boundary.

Setting boundaries allows a woman to express her displeasure with other people's negative emotions. It effectively stops the behaviour from continuing while being assertive/firm in communicating the consequences of further disrespect from others, thus creating an emotionally sound environment in which she can thrive.

Though it can prove uncomfortable at times, women must remember that a healthy, balanced lifestyle necessitates the establishment of clear boundaries.

Reflections

- *Are there situations for which you need to set boundaries?*
- *Give an example of a boundary you have set or would set for a given situation that makes you uncomfortable.*
- *Have you ever set a boundary and retrogressed because of overexplaining or felt guilty about your decision?*

5. When You Must Control Your Feelings

"*I am angry nearly every day!*" Jo, the feisty heroine of Louisa M Alcott's novel Little Women, exclaims. While anger isn't necessarily a bad thing in and of itself, being overwhelmed by it is!

Managing emotions so that they don't take over your life is a skill that everyone, especially women, should learn. Psychologists refer to this process as emotional regulation. Which helps understand your moving experiences and develop healthy coping mechanisms for difficult emotions.

Though beneficial, emotions may negatively impact interpersonal relationships and emotional health, especially when uncontrolled. Recognizing and managing your emotions is one of the most critical skills. It is essential to be able to feel and express feelings. They play an indispensable role in our reactions because they are our felt responses to a given situation. Being in tune with your emotions provides access to vital information for effective decision-making, relationship success, excellent self-care regimens, and greatly assists in day-to-day communication with others.

People who are good at noticing or acknowledging their emotions and can calmly communicate them to themselves and others are more likely to have healthy relationships and deal more effectively with setbacks and difficulties.

6. **Consider the Impact of Your Communication When Emotional**

Intense emotions aren't always destructive; they can indicate that we fully embrace life and are not suppressing our natural reactions. Feeling emotionally overwhelmed on occasion is normal and may occur when something wonderful or terrible happens or one feels like they have missed out.

When emotions are constantly out of control, it may indicate a problem that often results in strained relationships and conflict. This can lead to poor communication method choices like emotional outbursts that are either physical or verbal.

7. **When You Strive for Regulation Rather Than Repression**

Emotions cannot be switched on and off at will, though it would be great if one could manage them in that manner. When you suppress emotions, you stop yourself from freely feeling and expressing them consciously (suppression) or unconsciously (repression). This lack of expressive communication may lead to various mental and physical health symptoms.

To effectively control your emotions, ensure that you do not simply sweep them under the carpet but strive to communicate them without being overwhelmed by the emotion. This is essential for your healthy emotional well-being.

8. To Check in with Yourself

Taking a few moments to check in with yourself about your mood can assist you in regaining control. When suffering from anxiety or depression, it is common to feel that you have no control over your emotions.

Emotions can appear out of nowhere and be perplexing if they are stronger than you believe they should be in light of the current situation. For instance, you start crying after watching a sad movie because it was so moving or when you're enraged simply because your partner didn't take out the trash, but they did the week before.

Case Reflections

Here's a typical emotion communication situation adapted from Crystal Raypole:

Assume you've been dating someone for a few months. You tried to set up a date, but they said they didn't have time. You texted again the next day, saying, *"I'd like to see you soon." "Are you available to meet this week?"* After more than a day, they finally respond: *"Can't. Busy."* You become incredibly agitated and hurl your phone across the room, knock over your wastebasket, and kick your desk, stumbling over your toe.

Raypole suggests that to manage a situation like this, you need to interrupt yourself with the following questions:

1. What am I feeling at the moment? Is it disappointed, perplexed, or enraged?
2. What happened to make me feel this way? -They dismissed me without explanation.
3. Is there another explanation for the situation that might make sense? –Perhaps they're stressed, sick, or dealing with something else they don't want to talk about. They may intend to explain more when they are able.
4. What do I intend to do about these emotions? – Is screaming, throwing things, and texting something obnoxious the best response? Is there a better way to handle these emotions?
5. What if you ask the person if everything is fine and inquire about their next available day?
6. Do I need to calm down by taking a walk first?

Accepting emotions as they arise allows you to become more at ease with them. Increasing your comfort level in the presence of intense emotions will enable you to experience them without reacting in extreme, unhelpful ways entirely.

Asking similar questions like these will help you to reframe your thoughts by considering possible alternatives. This communication style can help you modify your initial extreme reaction. Though it may take some time for this response to become habitual, going through these steps in your head will become easier with practice. Best of all you will achieve emotional empowerment through it.

Reflections:

1. *Take some time to assess how your uncontrollable emotions affect your day-to-day life. This step will make identifying problem areas easier (and track your success).*

Final Take Away

Effective communication plays a big role in emotional empowerment. Learn to use it strategically both internally and with others for a more emotionally healthy and happy life.

CHAPTER 4:

HOW TO BE ASSERTIVE FOR EMOTIONAL EMPOWERMENT

Good news! being assertive doesn't have to be hard. You can adopt many helpful habits to make it easier as a woman, and in this chapter we will dive deeper into how to claim your emotional empowerment through assertiveness.

What is Being Assertive?

Being assertive means expressing your thoughts and feelings confidently and effectively. We all have the right to do this, but it can be hard for some people. Assertiveness involves "feeling" (or having a certain mindset about) something and then expressing that feeling with the appropriate words or actions in a given situation. It's not just about saying what you want - it's about doing it in a way that's respectful of everyone else too!

Many women struggle with being assertive because they have low self-esteem or feel anxiety. They tend to be awkward and they are known to have the following characteristics.

Characteristics of an Unassertive Woman

Being an unassertive woman is directly related to the type of man a woman needs. Unassertive women are willing to put up with a lot in relationships because they're afraid of standing up for themselves and being rejected if they do it. Here are some of the characteristics of an unassertive woman:

1. **They have self-doubting behaviour**

An unassertive woman will have a hard time looking at herself as someone worth having in her own right. She will also tend to view herself as a victim of her surroundings and circumstances, which forms the foundation for her tendency to please others and avoid conflict at all costs. This self-doubt will often lead a passive woman to seek out someone stronger, more confident, and more powerful than she is. Unfortunately, narcissists look for women that have self-doubt. The partners become like a godfather figure that she can rely on for strength, support and direction.

2. **They Live on Impression Management**

Unassertive women especially tend to put others' needs and wants above their own. She will continue to get along with them on her terms and will not raise her voice at all because she fears that she might be rejected. She may make an effort to please others, but chances are her best efforts will do nothing substantial in making the other person happy or satisfied. She may feel good about herself as she's doing it, but it's a misguided "goodness" that does little to produce true happiness or fulfilment in her life.

3. They Do Not Communicate Their Needs

Unassertive women also tend to be more passive in the manner they communicate their feelings to others. They will tend to be more indirect than direct in their approach as well, which makes it difficult for other people to understand where they stand on certain issues.

Benefits of Assertiveness

1. Improved self-confidence

Confident women draw others to them because they feel good about themselves. Being assertive helps a woman to be more confident in herself.

2. Improved Relationships with others

Assertiveness will help you to recognize relationships between yourself and other people, especially in situations where you are around friends, family members and coworkers. You will also know how to solve problems that may arise in your relationship with others when you are assertive with them, refusing to let your emotions get the best of you.

3. Improved Relationships with Yourself

Being assertive with yourself is about being honest about who you are and what you want from life for yourself. You need to know what your wants and needs are, how you want them met and how much control you want over them before deciding to go after them. Assertiveness will help you understand what your feelings are and how to handle them.

4. Improved Mental Health

Being assertive about yourself is about being honest with yourself about how you feel, what you want and also showing how strong you are inside by letting others know that your mind is strong enough not to let people take over control of your life.

5. Better Communication Skills

You need to be able to express yourself clearly and assertively so that other people will understand where they stand with you.

6. It Creates a Positive Outlook

When you are assertive, you can create your reality and this means that you have considerably more control over what happens in your life. Being assertive helps a person to be more positive about himself or herself because it opens up the doors to creating new perspectives. The woman can also see opportunities and take advantage of them instead of dwelling on the negative or what may have been.

7. It Stops Loser Behaviour

Behaviour that is not assertive includes all kinds of giving in, such as being passive-aggressive, manipulative and aggressive. These kinds of behaviour may occur when a woman is feeling insecure or weak about herself.

An assertive woman is a happier woman because she can safely express herself without hurting others.

Habits You Can Adopt to Become Assertive

1. **Change of Mindset**

Everyone has the right to be assertive (even if it's difficult). Recognizing this can help women feel more comfortable expressing themselves. The best way to be assertive is to express your feelings in a way that won't hurt anyone else. Be aware of your feelings and how to react to people. Sometimes it's hard to express oneself, but it will get easier with practice!

To practice assertiveness, start small and use a 'behavioural experiment.' For example, you might ask a co-worker or friend for help or try something outside your comfort zone. Then notice your feelings and how you reacted afterwards. When we feel anxious or doubtful about our actions, it can be helpful to reassure ourselves with positive statements. For example: *"I have the right to be assertive"* or *"I can do this."* You can also listen to yourself and find what you want; this will help you decide what is best for you.

Instead of thinking of a situation as scary- like speaking up in class, try thinking of it as challenging- like learning a new skill. Being assertive in that situation will feel more empowering and enjoyable, which is important if you want to keep practicing!

2. **Create Realistic Expectations**

If you expect too much from yourself, it may be hard to be assertive. When people expect too much from themselves, they focus on the things that can't be done, like speaking up in class or approaching a new person. Instead, focus on what you can do; like noticing an opportunity to support someone else or something you've always wanted to do. To help yourself with this, set realistic expectations: "*I will be assertive in X situation*" and "*I'll practice being assertive in Y situation.*"

To practice and build confidence in yourself, think of a time when you did something despite it being difficult or even though your feelings may have been mixed. Then think of two realistic ways you might have felt about doing it (one negative and one positive) for example, when you did math problems in class, and you felt frustrated. The negative way to feel was, "*I'm so stupid – why do I even bother!*" While the positive way was, "*I'm glad to improve my skills.*" Then think of a goal that's hard to be assertive about like approaching a stranger or meeting someone outside your comfort zone. Come up with a few realistic, positive expectations for each situation.

For example: "When I approach someone, I'll feel nervous but will try to stay calm." "I'll get tips from my friends on how they meet new people. I'll practice this until it feels easier."

Notice what you might want to do and why you feel scared or nervous. That's an important first step! If you are unsure, ask people who can help: a friend, an online forum, or your doctor.

Remember that talking to someone can sometimes be helpful, even if it doesn't solve the problem immediately! -Even when we don't feel like talking to people, telling our story can sometimes make us feel better.

It is also helpful to tell yourself that, "*I have the right to make my wants known.*" Try writing in a journal, "*I am assertive - I have the right to express my thoughts and feelings.*"

Focus on how your actions can be helpful - telling people what you want may help them too. For example, if someone is stressed out at work, you can suggest ways they can do tasks more effectively.

Actions That Can Help Women to Become Assertive

These assertive communication tips can help you become more assertive.

1. Speak up when you want to even if it hurts. You have the right to do this, and it's normal!
2. Group with other people and talk about your concerns. This might be easier than speaking up alone. For example: "there is a lot of work on our project right now but we can discuss how to plan and organize."
3. Assertiveness is more than just being assertive to others. It's also about being assertive with yourself. Take time to notice your thoughts, feelings, and needs. It can be helpful to tell yourself: *"I'll try to recognize these situations more"* or "I can tell myself, *"That's okay; I don't have to do everything!"*
4. It is also helpful to identify what makes you feel good about yourself. This will help you remember how it feels and help you get there again. Even if it's hard, you can tell yourself, *"This is hard for me but I can try."*
5. Try asking for what you want in a direct and specific way. For example, say to a friend, *"I'm frustrated with these assignments – could you help us organize them?"*
6. Stay flexible! Adapting to what's going on is a great way to be assertive. For example, if you want someone to make a change, ask how they could do it.

7. Try giving people choices instead of telling them what to do. For example: "*I was wondering how we could prepare for this test. Would you like to study tonight or tomorrow morning?*"
8. This might be a good time to start a daily journal. Writing in it can help you recognize your thoughts, feelings, and needs. Many women often find this helpful. Try to write at least three times per day: after you wake up, before going to bed, and sometime during the day (like during lunch). In your journal, pay attention to what you are thinking and feeling.
9. Try starting each entry with something like, "*I am feeling annoyed because...*" or "*I have some concerns about...*"
10. It can be helpful to ask yourself, "*What is it that I want?*" Then, go ahead and talk about it! For example, "*I worry that I'll never be assertive, but right now I'm feeling...This is hard for me but I can try.*" or "*I need a chance to express my ideas.*" Notice the way you feel when you notice these feelings and what makes you feel good about yourself.
11. Speak up in class, around your friends, and at work. It's okay if you are nervous; remember these tips and keep trying!

Reflections

1. *How can being assertive help you in your current life?*
2. *Do you believe assertiveness will help you develop a sense of independence and self-reliance?*
3. *What steps can you take towards being assertive in your relationships, work or social life?*

How Women Can Practice Assertiveness in Different Situations.

If you are a woman who is tired of feeling submissive, incompetent and unable to stand up for herself in different situations, here is a list of six tips to help empower you and help you adopt an assertive mindset in your life.

1. **Establish clear boundaries with others.**

The first step to becoming an assertive woman lies within yourself. Learn how to create a personal space and also be able to say no when somebody asks something out of your abilities or comfort zone.

2. **Stop internalizing the demands of others (including negative attitudes).**

Learn how to separate your perceptions from the viewpoint of others. Noticing your reaction to certain situations will help you see how you are imposing the demand of others upon yourself.

3. **Notice when you feel like a victim and why.**

It's crucial to understand that any situation can be perceived differently. For example, many women who are victims of abuse in relationships might feel hopeless and think about their circumstances as outside of their control. This mindset prevents them from taking action to improve their situations because they have already decided that it is hopeless.

4. **Practice being assertive (in a controlled way).**

Becoming an assertive woman is not easy and is not something that you can do overnight. You have to practice being assertive in situations that don't matter. Be mindful of what you are saying and how you respond to others. By practicing this exercise, you will eventually be able to bring your assertiveness into critical situations, such as when you need to speak up for yourself at work or disagree with your partner's opinion at home.

5. **Ask for help from an objective source.**

If your situation requires serious action, then ask the advice of a close friend or trusted family member who will offer a different perspective on the problem. Accepting their advice is not the same as accepting their criticism. For example, if you face humiliation from your husband and he does not seem to change, it is wise to engage someone from his family to talk to him and find a solution.

6. **Take responsibility for what you can personally control and then forget about it.**

There are certain situations in life that we cannot control. Other people's actions are a perfect example of what you cannot control. What you can control is your reaction to those events; therefore, focus on the things that matter to you as a woman. Accept the situation and do your best to improve it by taking action or asking for help. Every small step moves you towards improving your situation.

Final Take Away

Unassertive women may come across as shy or meek, while an assertive woman is self-assured and knows her mind. Being assertive can empower women; it gives them a voice and makes them feel confident in themselves. If you're uncomfortable being overtly assertive, start small by expressing your opinions more often or refusing to do something you don't want to do. With time and practice, you'll find that asserting yourself comes more naturally and you are more emotionally empowered.

CHAPTER 5:

CELEBRATING EMOTIONAL EMPOWERMENT IN WOMEN

Building emotional empowerment is an important part of a woman's life. Without it, she can feel like she lacks control and strength in her life. In this chapter, we shall look at all the wonderful things an emotionally empowered woman is and can be.

Emotional empowerment is beneficial for both women and the people around them, so let's celebrate it! Here are the reasons why!

1. **An Emotionally Empowered Woman Creates an Empowered Society.**

There is increasing evidence that the more emotionally balanced society is the more successful and harmonious it is. The effort to re-empower women in our societies has a long history and is boldly evident today. Let's take, for instance, Winfrey Oprah- who was defiled by close family members but rose to prominence by using her story to inspire generations of women that she sponsors and educates for their empowerment. Actress, Angelina Jolie, despite being a superstar, had the interests of the less privileged at heart and turned her influence into helping thousands of people. These and many other women have blossomed in proving that by nurturing both positive and negative emotions despite different setbacks in life, goodness and impact can be created. These emotionally empowered women must be celebrated because they go against the grain of how the majority population would have reacted to pain and suffering- which is to take a victim mentality.

2. An Emotionally Empowered Woman Honours Her Femininity

One misconception that is mostly believed in society is that to be powerful, one must adopt masculine traits. Well, the fact is that true powers come from balancing masculine and feminine energies. An empowered woman respectfully honours and embraces her feminine and masculine traits.

3. An Emotionally Empowered Woman Speaks Her Mind.

Women who speak their minds are said to be rude and intimidating, but a woman needs to speak the truth. Many women in the world are told that it is un-feminine to share their ideas, consciously or subconsciously, and more so if the ideas contradict or threaten others. However, the feminine point of view is an important and integral part of the balance in society. Women will never lose their femininity by expressing one's thoughts, opinions or ideas honestly.

In the book *A Woman's Worth,* Marianne Williamson stated, "Women will still be in emotional bondage as long as we need to worry that we have to choose between being heard and loved." Therefore, we celebrate emotional balance and women's empowerment because it allows women to be heard.

4. An Emotionally Empowered Woman Leads with Love.

People believe that a woman has to fight for respect, power and leadership, but an ideal empowered woman knows that leading with love is the strongest power source. Emotionally empowered women use love as their main motivation when they lead; they also incorporate the many facets of love, i.e., compassion, patience, empathy and self-love, into their actions. For example, beyond all odds, Kate Winslet, an American actress, lends her support to several charities with financial donations. She also became the patron of a Gloucester-based charity, the Family Haven, which provides counselling services to vulnerable families. All these activities were done with love and compassion as the end goal.

5. Emotionally Empowered Woman Finds Balance.

Balance plays a key role in tapping into one's natural power source. We all carry masculine and feminine energies but, naturally, tend towards one more than the other. Each individual has unique personality traits. To understand and embrace our natural energies, we must work towards equal respect for our opposing energies, as both are necessary for a fully functioning existence. Despite being a media personality, Orpah was also an actress and a co-author. She balanced all these and is labelled as one of the most powerful and influential women in the world today.

6. An Emotionally Empowered Woman is Authentic.

Once a woman is empowered and emotionally balanced, she does not need to pretend to be someone else as she is always herself. She always respects and honours herself, honours her feminine or masculine powers and practices authenticity.

In authenticity lies the greatest strength and influence. Being authentic does not waste energy, leaving more space and energy to effect real change and results in the here and now. For example, when Naomi Osaka decided to quit the tennis world, she was very authentic when she said, "The truth remains I have suffered depression in the U.S. Open since 2018 and I have had a hard time coping with that." Osaka's admission of emotional drain showed how authentic she was, making her a celebrated champion to this date.

Reflections

1. *What is the key message you have taken from these aspects of celebrating emotionally empowered women?*
2. *What 3 steps can you take towards being an emotionally empowered woman in your life today?*

Final Take Away

Life is a roller coaster and we cannot control the hand we are dealt. However, we can control how we feel about these situations to make the best out of them. The cup is either half full or half empty based on perspective. However, emotional empowerment is more than just positive thinking it's being emotionally intelligent and mature enough. Once you actualize emotional empowerment, it's a journey worth celebrating!

CHAPTER 6:

YOUR EMOTIONAL INTELLIGENCE QUIZ

Do you sometimes feel like you're not in control of your emotions? Like they take over and you can't seem to do anything about it? If so, this emotion analysis quiz is perfect for you! It will help you manage your emotions better and figure out how to deal with them healthily. So, what are you waiting for? Take the quiz now!

How Emotionally Intelligent Are You? Take the Quiz!

Emotionally intelligent people are aware of their feelings and can use that knowledge to better themselves and their communities. Can you get smart about your feelings? This is the consensus of specialists. Enhancing emotional intelligence is a lifelong process. Everyone knows someone who has their feelings under complete control. They keep their cool under pressure and act responsibly even when things look bleak. Some women you might know can also read the feelings of those around them. They know what to say to lift people's spirits and motivate them to take action. These people have a high level of emotional intelligence (or EI). They can keep their cool in tense situations and maintain solid friendships. People with these traits are also likely to be able to bounce back quickly after experiencing setbacks. How emotionally intelligent are you, and where do you have room to grow? Try out the emotional intelligence quiz below to find out.

1. Two of your close friends are fighting against each other. What do you do?
   - Sit them down and let them understand each other's viewpoint
   - Choose one side and talk badly about the other friend
   - Escape from the fighting scene until the fight is over
   - Allow them to vent their emotions for you to listen

2. One of your friends has informed you of the unfortunate event of suffering a miscarriage. How do you respond?
   - Give your friend a chance to express how they feel, then offer your support.
   - Advise her to have a few friends over and clear her mind through partying.
   - Give her time on her own to process the whole thing.
   - Spend time with her but not engage in the tragic event that has just happened to her.

3. Whenever you are facing or handling an unpleasant task, what do you tend to do?
   - Have a plan and work on it each day, little by little.
   - Wait until the last minute to complete the task
   - Get it done as quickly as possible.
   - Avoid handling or doing the task at all.

4. Your baby girl throws a tantrum in the supermarket because you have refused to buy her candy. What do you do?
    - Try and engage her and find out how she is feeling.
    - Ignore her while she is throwing tantrums and crying.
    - Get her the candy she is crying over and cool her down
    - Quickly get your belongings and run away from the supermarket.

5. When engaging in heated arguments, what do you usually do?
    - Ask for breaks from the arguments before resuming the discussion.
    - Apologize as soon as possible to avoid the argument.
    - Throw insults at the person you are in an argument with.
    - Shut down completely and not respond to the other person.

6. What do you do when making the most important decisions?
    - I follow my instincts.
    - I tend to go with the option that seems easiest
    - Ask for directions from other people
    - Make random guesses

7. Which of these statements can perfectly describe who you are?
    - I have an easy time interacting with new people, getting to know them and turning them into friends.

- o I take my time and know someone before considering them a true friend
- o I find it difficult to interact with people and make friends.
- o Maintaining close friendships is an uphill task for me

8. You have just gotten a bad grade on a subject you have worked hard to prepare for. How do you handle it?
   - o Try and think of ways you can work towards improving the project.
   - o Reach out to the professor and confront them for a better grade
   - o Criticize the work you had put in and say how you could have done better
   - o Negatively view the class and stop putting effort into that subject

9. Your colleague at work has a habit that you find annoying and doesn't seem to stop. What do you do?
   - o Approach the colleague and tell them how it is bothering you
   - o File a formal complaint to your immediate supervisor
   - o Talk to your other colleagues about how you are feeling about the colleague without their knowledge
   - o Endure the whole thing in silence

10. You already feel the pressure of being overworked in the office, and your boss hands you a new project. How do you feel?
    - o A sense of anxiety about how to get the project done.
    - o The feeling of being overwhelmed by the task at hand.

- o Anger towards your boss for not being observant enough to see how overworked you are.
- o Depressed and sure that you may never finish the task given

11. Are you aware of how your moods change from time to time?

- o Never
- o Rarely
- o Sometimes
- o Always

12. Do you know the things that affect your mood or make you angry and sad from time to time?

- o Never
- o Rarely
- o Sometimes
- o Always

13. Do you grasp why you feel sad, angry or happy every time?

- o Never
- o Rarely
- o Sometimes
- o Always

14. Are you aware of the moments when your emotions are affecting your performance?

- o No, Never
- o Not Often
- o Sometimes

- Always

15. How fast do you know that you are losing your temper?

    - Very Slowly
    - Slowly
    - Quite Quickly
    - Very Quickly

16. How fast do you realize that your self-talk is no longer positive?

    - Usually Too Late
    - After Awhile
    - Quite Soon
    - Straight Away

17. How regularly do you worry about things that rarely happen?

    - Often
    - Sometimes
    - Rarely
    - Never

18. How well can you say you keep your concentration when you have anxiety?

    - Not At All
    - Just About
    - Quite Well
    - Very Well

19. Is it possible for you to tell when you are being defensive?

    - Never

- o Rarely
- o Sometimes
- o Always

20. Are you always relaxed when you are facing pressure?

    - o Not At All
    - o Hardly Ever
    - o Quite Easily
    - o Very Easily

21. Is it easy to have things going when you are frustrated?

    - o Never
    - o Not Usually
    - o Sometimes
    - o Usually

22. Do you tend to remain calm when handling people who are angry around you?

    - o Never
    - o Occasionally
    - o Usually
    - o Always

23. How often can you say that you feel empathetic to other people's issues?

    - o Never
    - o Rarely
    - o Sometimes
    - o Always

24. Is it possible for you to feel when other people are anxious and respond promptly?
    - o Never
    - o Hardly Ever
    - o Yes, Often
    - o Yes, Always

25. Can you help other people boost their morale when they are feeling frustrated?
    - o Never
    - o Not Often
    - o Yes, Sometimes
    - o Yes, Often

26. How freely could you say that you offer help to other people?
    - o Not Freely at All
    - o Reluctantly
    - o Quite Freely
    - o Very Freely

27. How effectively could you say that you share your feelings with others?
    - o Not At All
    - o Not Very
    - o Quite
    - o Very

28. Are you good at making conversations and making people be at ease?
    - o Not At All

- o Not Very
- o Quite
- o Very

29. How good can you say you are at offering constructive criticism that will not cause conflict?

    - o Not Good at All
    - o Not So Good
    - o Fairly Good
    - o Very Good

30. When in a workgroup or home setup, how often do you help people solve conflicts?

    - o Never
    - o Rarely
    - o Sometimes
    - o Often

31. To what extent would you say you can persuade people to follow your lead?

    - o None
    - o Very Little
    - o To Some Extent
    - o A Great Extent

32. If someone is unwilling to openly share their feeling and thoughts, how willing can you be to talk on their behalf?

    - o Not At All Willing
    - o Quite Reluctantly
    - o Can Be Persuaded
    - o Very Willing

33. Suppose there are changes in circumstances or relationships; how willing would you be to accept the change?
    - o Not At All Willing
    - o Quite Reluctantly
    - o Can Be Persuaded
    - o Very Willing

34. To what extent would you say that other people find you trustworthy and can confide in you?
    - o Never
    - o Hardly Ever
    - o Occasionally
    - o Frequently

35. Do you know clearly what drives you as a person?
    - o Not At All
    - o Just About
    - o Quite Well
    - o Very Well

36. Would you say that you can bounce back quickly after facing a setback?
    - o Never
    - o Rarely
    - o Quite Often
    - o Without Fail

37. Do you find it easy to keep promises?
    - o No, Never
    - o Not Often
    - o Yes, Sometimes

- o Yes, Always

38. Would you say that you would change your methods if your current methods are not bringing the desired results?

    - o Very Reluctantly
    - o Quite Reluctantly
    - o Quite Willingly
    - o Very Willingly

39. How well would you say that you understand your purpose in life?

    - o Never
    - o Hardly
    - o Quite Well
    - o Very Well

40. How frequently do you set EQ goals for yourself?

    - o Never
    - o Rarely
    - o Sometimes
    - o Always

That's it! You've completed the emotional intelligence quiz. Now what? Visit this website, by the Global Leadership Foundation to see how you scored and get personalized tips on how to improve your emotional intelligence. We hope that this quiz has helped you learn a little more about yourself and the way you interact with others. Thanks for taking the time to do it!

CONCLUSION

Congratulations on making it this far!

You now know that being an emotionally empowered woman means being in touch with your emotions and using them to empower yourself. It's about understanding all about emotions - their triggers, how they manifest themselves and what you can do to manage them effectively. Emotionally empowered women know that their feelings are a powerful tool that they can use to navigate through life successfully. And while the path to emotional empowerment is not always easy, the rewards are more than worth it. Just think of some of the most successful and famous women in history - many of whom were emotionally empowered individuals. There are countless examples, but here are just a few: Oprah Winfrey, Hillary Clinton, Graca Machel and many others. Each woman has used her emotional intelligence to achieve great things in life.

Use and keep this guide close knowing that you must take small, meaningful, and sustainable steps to form a habit. Therefore, resist the urge to try to tackle everything all at once. Make self-care a priority even if you don't think you have time for anything else! The most crucial aspect of all of this is to be gentle with yourself. Also, be assertive and don't let others walk all over you or control your life. Most of all empathize with others to foster strong relationships.

Keep growing and do not underestimate your strengths as a woman. Live authentically, live an emotionally empowered life!

Thanks again for reading this book

Connect with me:

Instagram: @IAMDREVELYNOKPANACHI
Website: www.evelynokpanachi.com

Wishing you love,
Evelyn Okpanachi

REFERENCES

Eanne Segal, P. M. (n.d.). *Improving Emotional Intelligence (EQ)*. Retrieved from HelpGuide: https://www.helpguide.org/articles/mental-health/emotional-intelligence-eq.htm

ONELOVE. (n.d.). *5 Easy Ways To Communicate Better in Your Relationship*. Retrieved from onelove: https://www.joinonelove.org/learn/5-easy-ways-to-communicate-better-in-your-relationships/

Seconds, S. (n.d.). *Take Your Free Emotional Intelligence Test*. Retrieved from Six seconds: https://www.6seconds.org/freetest/

Today, P. (n.d.). *Emotional Intelligence Test*. Retrieved from Psychology Today: https://www.psychologytoday.com/us/tests/personality/emotional-intelligence-test

Tools, M. (n.d.). *How Emotionally Intelligent Are You?* Retrieved from Mind Tools: https://www.mindtools.com/axbwm3m/how-emotionally-intelligent-are-you

Diskal, L. (2016). *Understand assertiveness.2. Keep your communication style in line.3. Understand and accept.* Inc. Africa. https://incafrica.com/library/lolly-daskal-7-powerful-habits-that-make-you-more-assertive.

Angelina Jolie's Impressive Emotional Intelligence And Humanitarian Work. (2022, April 29). The Inquisitr. https://www.inquisitr.com/10006525/angelina-jolies-impressive-emotional-intelligence-and-humanitar

Firelight and Graça Machel on making a better future for Africa's women and children. (n.d.). Firelight Foundation. Retrieved November 17, 2022, from https://www.firelightfoundation.org/blog/2017/08/22/firelight-and-graca-machel-on-making-a-better-future-for-africas-women-and-children

First Lady Michelle Obama. (2009). The White House. https://obamawhitehouse.archives.gov/realitycheck/node/357156

Hougaard, R., Carter, J., Coutts, G. (2016). Emotional Balance. In: One Second Ahead. Palgrave Macmillan, New York. https://doi.org/10.1057/9781137551924_16

Home - workplace strategies for Mental Health. WSMH. (n.d.). Retrieved March 22, 2022, from https://www.workplacestrategiesformentalhealth.com/resources/emotional-triggers

Tlalka, S., Rossy, L., Whitney-Coulter, A., Naidoo, U., & Smookler, E. (2021, November 23). *Find happiness by embracing all of your emotions.* Mindful. Retrieved March 22, 2022, from https://www.mindful.org/want-pursue-happiness-embrace-emotions/

India Today Digital. (2012, April 11). *5 steps to emotional empowerment*. India Today. Retrieved March 22, 2022, from https://www.indiatoday.in/prevention/story/5-steps-to-emotional-empowerment-98784-2012-04-11

Nast, C. (2014, April 4). *Kate Winslet's work/life balance: "It's alright for some."* Glamour U.K. https://www.glamourmagazine.co.uk/article/kate-winslet-on-her-work-life-balance-its-alright-for-some

Santos, J. (2015, June 24). *The stigma of being an emotional woman.* But First, Joy. Retrieved April 12, 2022, from https://butfirstjoy.com/stigma-emotional-woman/

How Emotions Affect Behaviour. (2016, June 28). Retrieved from https://study.com/academy/lesson/how-emotions-affect-behaviour.html

Carpentier, M. (2016, September 29). *Hillary Clinton was cheated on and stayed. Many of us do the same.* The Guardian. Retrieved April 12, 2022, from https://www.theguardian.com/us-news/2016/sep/29/hillary-clinton-cheating-husband-stayed-women

Ludovino, E. M. (2017, January 26). *EMOTIONAL EMPOWERMENT - Are you emotionally empowered?* Retrieved from LinkedIn: https://www.linkedin.com/pulse/emotional-empowerment-you-empowered-emotional-intelligence-coach/

Nast, C. (2017, March 23). *Kate Winslet Reveals She was Bullied for Her Weight as a Child.* SELF. https://www.self.com/story/kate-winslet-bullied

Coleman, D. V. (2018, March 3). *What makes an empowered woman?* Stand InBalance. Retrieved November 19, 2022, from https://standinbalance.com/empowered-woman/

Steinhilber, B. (2018, July 24). *Is your emotional baggage holding you back?* NBCNews.com. Retrieved March 22, 2022, from https://www.nbcnews.com/better/health/your-emotional-baggage-holding-you-back-ncna877596

Human and Hope Association. (2018, August 28). *Why women's empowerment is so important?* https://www.humanandhopeassociation.org/2018/02/02/womens-empowerment-important/

Fletcher, T. L. (2019, February 19). *Improve Work Relationships Through Empowering Communication.* Retrieved from TERRALFLETCHER.COM: https://terralfletcher.com/improve-work-relationships-through-empowering-communication/

Devlin, H. (2019, May 12). *Science of anger: How gender, age and personality shape this emotion.* The Guardian. Retrieved March 22, 2022, from https://www.theguardian.com/lifeandstyle/2019/may/12/science-of-anger-gender-age-personality

Tables, S. (2019, May 24). *Https://www.collinsdictionary.com/dictionary/english-thesaurus.* Medium. Retrieved March 22, 2022, from https://medium.com/@anonmilzee/https-www-collinsdictionary-com-dictionary-english-thesaurus-429319f9a0bd

Martin, S. (2019, June 18). *5 tips for setting boundaries with ease.* Live Well with Sharon Martin. Retrieved March 22, 2022, from https://www.livewellwithsharonmartin.com/tips-for-setting-boundaries/5-tips-for-setting-boundaries-with-ease/

Pietrangelo, A. (2019, October 28). *How to handle a narcissist: 9 tips.* Healthline. https://www.healthline.com/health/how-to-deal-with-a-narcissist#Watch-more-from-the-Youth-in-Focus-video-series

Morzaria, H. (2019, December 1). *The different types of emotions and how they impact human behaviour.* Business 2 Community. Retrieved March 22, 2022, from https://www.business2community.com/workplace-culture/the-different-types-of-emotions-and-how-they-impact-human-behaviour-02263872

Lamothe, C. (2020, March 30). *Are you emotionally mature?* Healthline. Retrieved April 9, 2022, from https://www.healthline.com/health/mental-health/emotional-maturity#age-and-other-factors

Raypole, C. (2020, April 28). *How to control your emotions: 11 strategies to try.* Healthline. Retrieved April 7, 2022, from https://www.healthline.com/health/how-to-control-your-emotions

Cherry, K. (2020, July 13). 9 signs of low emotional intelligence. Verywell Mind. Retrieved April 11, 2022, from https://www.verywellmind.com/signs-of-low-emotional-intelligence-2795958

5 keys to emotional empowerment. Exploring your mind. (2020, September 25). Retrieved April 11, 2022, from https://exploringyourmind.com/5-keys-emotional-empowerment/

The Chelsea Psychology Clinic. (2020, October 2). *What are my needs? identifying your emotional needs in a relationship.* The Chelsea Psychology Clinic. Retrieved April 11, 2022, from https://www.thechelseapsychologyclinic.com/sex-relationships/what-are-my-needs/

Raypole, C., & Linter, J. (2020, November 13). *Emotional triggers: Definition and how to manage them.* Healthline. Retrieved March 21, 2022, from https://www.healthline.com/health/mental-health/emotional-triggers#coping-in-the-momen

Byrne, J. (2020, December 10). *The importance of managing expectations.* LinkedIn. Retrieved April 9, 2022, from https://www.linkedin.com/pulse/importance-managing-expectations-justin-byrne

Oberlo. (2020, December 10). *A quick summary of The 7 Habits of Highly Effective People.* Oberlo | Where Self Made is Made. https://www.oberlo.com/blog/7-habits-of-highly-effective-people-by-stephen-covey-summary

She. (2021, April 13). *Emotional maturity = healthy relationships.* she. Retrieved April 9, 2022, from https://shiftingherexperience.com/emotional-maturity-healthy-relationships/

sleeves, o. o. (2021, May). *What is Emotional Empowerment?* Retrieved from On our sleeves:

https://www.onoursleeves.org/mental-wellness-tools-guides/emotional-development/emotional-empowerment

Jensen, E. (2021, May 20). *"The Me You Can't See"*: Oprah talks about being molested as a child and breaks down in tears. USA TODAY. https://www.usatoday.com/story/entertainment/tv/2021/05/21/oprah-the-me-you-cant-see-talks-rape-and-trauma/5186682001/

Cherry, K. (2021, July 14). *The important role of emotions.* Verywell Mind. Retrieved March 22, 2022, from https://www.verywellmind.com/the-purpose-of-emotions-2795181

Elmer, J. (2021, September 9). *Why am I so emotional? 15 reasons you're feeling extra sensitive.* Healthline. Retrieved March 22, 2022, from https://www.healthline.com/health/why-am-i-so-emotional-2

Brett & Kate McKay. (2021, September 25). *Quit being a pushover: How to be assertive.* The Art of Manliness. https://www.artofmanliness.com/people/social-skills/how-to-be-assertive/

Robbins, M. (2021, September 30). *Your feelings matter: How to embrace your emotions.* Mike Robbins | Infusing Life and Business with Authenticity and Appreciation. Retrieved April 13, 2022, from https://mike-robbins.com/your-feelings-matter/

Cherry, K. (2021, October 11). *How Emotionally Intelligent Are You?* Retrieved from Verywell mind: https://www.verywellmind.com/how-emotionally-intelligent-are-you-2796099

Morin, A. (2021, November 29). *Healthy coping skills for uncomfortable emotions.* Verywell Mind. Retrieved April 11, 2022, from https://www.verywellmind.com/forty-healthy-coping-skills-4586742

KeyStep Media. (2022, January 14). *What is emotional balance? (And how to cultivate it) - key step media.* Key Step Media - Leadership, Mindfulness, Emotional Intelligence. Retrieved April 13, 2022, from https://www.keystepmedia.com/emotional-balance/

HelpGuide. (2022, February 8). Improving emotional intelligence (EQ). *HelpGuide.org.* Retrieved April 11, 2022, from https://www.helpguide.org/articles/mental-health/emotional-intelligence-eq.htm

Fritscher, L. (2022, February 10). The psychology behind Fear. Very well Mind. Retrieved March 22, 2022, from https://www.verywellmind.com/the-psychology-of-fear-2671696

Hood, J. (2022, February 25). *The benefits and importance of a support system: Highland Springs Clinic.* Highland Springs. Retrieved April 13, 2022, from https://highlandspringsclinic.org/blog/the-benefits-and-importance-of-a-support-system/#:~:text=Researchers%20have%20also%20said%20that,and%20anxiety%20and%20reduce%20stress.

American Behavioural Clinics. (2022, February 28). *10 signs of emotional maturity.* American Behavioural Clinics. Retrieved April 10, 2022, from https://americanbehaviouralclinics.com/10-signs-of-emotional-maturity/

V, J. (2022, March 21). *16 'habits' of highly emotional people.* The Mighty. Retrieved March 22, 2022, from https://themighty.com/2019/08/habits-of-highly-eonal-people/

The three types of Fear. (n.d.). Retrieved March 22, 2022, from https://escapegames.ca/three-types-of-fear/

Hussain, A. (2022, April 11). *7 habits of highly effective people [Summary & takeaways].* HubSpot Blog | Marketing, Sales, Agency, and Customer Success Content. https://blog.hubspot.com/sales/habits-of-highly-effective-people-summary

Mayo Clinic Staff. (2022, May 13). *Stressed out? Be assertive.* Mayo Clinic. https://www.mayoclinic.org/healthy-lifestyle/stress-management/in-depth/assertive/art-20044644

Martins, J. (2022, August 31). *Emotional intelligence: 9 strategies to improve EQ in the workplace.* Retrieved from Asana: https://asana.com/resources/emotional-intelligence-skills

Morin, A. (2022, October 12). 7 things mentally strong women believe. Forbes. Retrieved November 19, 2022, from https://www.forbes.com/sites/amymorin/2020/02/11/7-things-mentally-strong-women-believe/?sh=14ab04041b4e

Inc.Africa. (n.d.). Incafrica.com. Retrieved November 17, 2022, from https://incafrica.com/library/bill-murphy-jr-people-who-admit-these-3-brutal-truths-have-very-high-emotional-intelligence-examples-oprah-winfrey-kate-winslet-naomi-osaka

Emotional balance. HandsOn. (n.d.). Retrieved November 19, 2022, from https://www.handsonscotland.co.uk/emotional-balance/

The kit. IFF Praxis RSS. (n.d.). Retrieved November 19, 2022, from http://www.iffpraxis.com/kitbag-kit

Franklin Convey. (2022, November 23). *The-7-habits.* Franklin Covey. https://www.franklincovey.com/the-7-habits/

Printed in Great Britain
by Amazon